Science for All Seasons
Summer

Grades PreK-K

Project Manager:
Michele M. Dare

Writers:
Lucia Kemp Henry
Dr. Suzanne Moore

Contributing Editors:
Cindy K. Daoust, Jayne Gammons, Ada Goren, Sherri Lynn Kuntz

Art Coordinator:
Kimberly Richard

Artists:
Pam Crane, Teresa Davidson, Susan Hodnett,
Sheila Krill, Kimberly Richard, Greg D. Rieves,
Rebecca Saunders, Donna K. Teal

Cover Artists:
Nick Greenwood and Kimberly Richard

www.themailbox.com

©2000 by THE EDUCATION CENTER, INC.
All rights reserved.
ISBN #1-56234-382-3

Manufactured in the United States
10 9 8 7 6 5 4 3 2 1

Table of Contents

The World of Weather

Sunny Days

Center your weather studies around the forecast for the summer season—warm and sunny with an excellent chance for your little scientists to learn about the sun!

Sun Senses

Introduce your youngsters to some "sun-sational" science with this observational activity. In advance, cut a sun shape from a large sheet of yellow bulletin board paper. Write "A sunny day is…" across the top of the sun. Then take your little ones outside to observe the light. (Be sure to direct students *not* to look directly at the sun.) Have students find objects in direct sunlight and objects in the shade. Then have them compare the differences. Next, have students tightly close their eyes and face the sun. Invite them to describe what the summer sunshine feels like. After returning to the classroom, discuss students' observations. Lead students to conclude that the sun gives light and heat to the earth. Then ask each child to complete the phrase "A sunny day is…" Write his response on the sun-shaped chart. If desired, photograph each child in the sunshine. Then mount the sun chart and the photos on a bulletin board.

A sunny day is ...
hot
bright
fun
shiny

A sunny day is ...
hot
bright
fun
shiny

This Is Why

The cut glass in a prism bends the light shining through it. When the sunlight bends, or *refracts*, the different colors are revealed.

Somewhere Over the Rainbow

Did you know that every ray of light contains a rainbow? While sunlight appears to have no color of its own, it is actually made of many different colors. Use this simple small-group activity to reveal the sun's true colors. On a sunny day, spread a large white sheet on the ground. Then provide each child in the group with a prism. Have her hold the prism so that the light shines through it and projects a rainbow onto the sheet.

Feeling the Heat

Here's a hands-on investigation that will have your youngsters really feeling the heat! In advance, locate two sidewalks around your school—one that is in bright sunlight during the afternoon, and one that is in full shade. Take your youngsters to the shaded area and have them feel the surface with their hands. Invite each child to describe the temperature of the shaded surface. Next, take students to the sunny sidewalk and have them touch and describe it. Ask students to explain why the surface in the sunlight is hotter than the one in the shade. Lead students to conclude that the sun warmed the sidewalk.

Soaking Up Sunshine

Use this outdoor experiment to help your little ones soak up more information on the sun's heat. To prepare, lay one white and one black piece of construction paper in a sunny area outside. Anchor each piece of paper with a wooden block. After the papers have been in direct sunlight for a few hours, take your youngsters outside to examine the papers. Have students predict which paper will be warmer. Then invite each child, in turn, to feel the papers. Youngsters may be surprised to discover that the black paper is warmer than the white one!

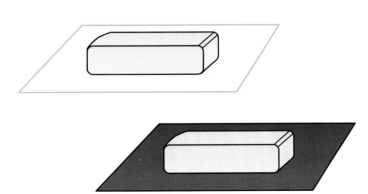

This Is Why

Objects that are dark in color *absorb* sunlight and heat up more readily. Objects that are light in color *reflect* more light and heat. The sunlight and heat mostly bounce off the light-colored object. This is why wearing light colors outside in the hot sunshine can keep you cooler than wearing dark colors.

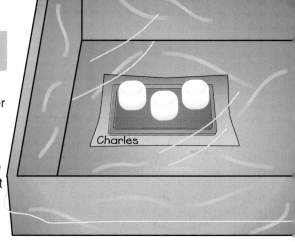

Sun S'mores

Use the heat of the sun to help create this tasty solar snack! To prepare, cover a large box with aluminum foil as shown. Then use a permanent marker to personalize a small piece of foil for each child. Next, provide each child with one fourth of a graham cracker, a thin piece of chocolate, and three miniature marshmallows. Direct him to place the cracker on his foil and then place the chocolate and marshmallows on the cracker. Set each snack inside the box and then cover the box with clear plastic wrap. Place the box in direct sunlight until the chocolate begins to melt. Remove the snacks from the box and eat! Yum!

Ice Cube Paintings

What else will melt in the hot summer sun? Ice! Use this nice ice activity to sharpen youngsters' observation skills and develop their artistic talent. To prepare, thoroughly mix six tablespoons of paint with five ounces of water. Then pour the mixture into one side of an ice cube tray. Repeat the previous two steps to fill the other side of the tray. Cover the tray with aluminum foil. Insert a craft stick through the foil into each cube and then freeze the cubes. When you're ready to use the cubes, dip the tray into warm water for a few seconds; then pop the cubes out of the tray.

To begin the activity, take children to a sunny area outside. Give each child a piece of white art paper and a tinted ice cube. Then direct her to paint with the cube. As the cube begins to melt in the sun, have students observe any changes in the lines and designs made by the cubes.

Melting in the Sun

Now that each child has discovered that the sun can melt chocolate and ice, help your little ones brainstorm a list of other foods that will melt in the sun. Write their responses on a chart. Then use each listed item in the song below.

It's Melting in the Sun!
(sung to the tune of "If You're Happy and You Know It")

It's melting in the sun, in the sun.
It's melting in the sun, in the sun.
It's [an ice cube], yes sirree,
Sitting in the sun, you see.
And it's melting, yes, it's melting in the sun!

Sing the song several more times, replacing the underlined phrase, in turn, with *chocolate* and other foods listed by the children.

5

Disappearing Designs

Did you know the sun can make water disappear? Use this small-group activity to amaze your youngsters and demonstrate the sun's role in *evaporation*. In advance, provide each child with a small spray bottle filled with water. Then take the group outside to a bright, sunny sidewalk. Demonstrate how to spray water on the sidewalk and create a design. Then have youngsters observe the design as it vanishes! Next, invite each child to use his bottle and create his own disappearing design. Is it magic? No, it's the sun!

This Is Why

When water is placed on a surface like a sidewalk, the heat of the sun causes the water to change into water vapor, which is a gas. The water vapor then rises into the air, causing the design to disappear! This process is called *evaporation*.

Did You Know?

Clouds are also formed through evaporation. When the sun heats water from oceans and lakes, the water evaporates and forms clouds!

Me and My Shadow

Presto! Change-o! Watch the shadow change! Help develop observation and thinking skills with this magical shadow activity. To prepare, find a paved outdoor area that receives a lot of sun throughout the day. Cover a large portion of the area with white bulletin board paper. Then mark the middle of the area with an X. In the morning, take your class outside and choose one child to stand on the X. Trace around the child's shadow with a marker and write the time of day inside the outline. Throughout the day, return to the area and repeat the previous step with the same child. At the end of the day, have children observe the differences in the shadows. Then have them guess why the shadows changed in size.

This Is Why

As the earth moves around the sun, the sun's position in the sky changes. The different positions cause the light to shine on the earth at different angles and create a variety of shadows.

2:30

1:30

12:30

11:30

10:30

The Power of Sunlight

Turn your youngsters on to the power of sunlight! Use this activity to show that sunlight can cause materials to fade. In advance, cut a tagboard sun shape for each child. Then provide each child with a sun and a personalized 5" x 7" sheet of dark blue, purple, or red construction paper. Have the child place her paper in the direct sunlight outside and then place her tagboard sun in the center of her paper. If necessary, anchor the paper by placing a small block on the tagboard sun. Set each child's paper in the sunlight until the paper has faded. Then have the child remove the tagboard sun from her paper and observe the changes. Lead students to conclude that the sunlight caused the paper to fade. After discussing the power of sunlight, have students use their sun-faded papers as covers for their Red-Hot Sun booklets on page 8.

Note: Some papers will fade faster than others. For best results, use inexpensive construction paper.

This Is Why

When light shines on some colored papers, it causes a chemical change that makes the paper fade. When the sun shape is placed on top of the colored paper in the experiment, the shape blocks the paper beneath it from exposure to sunlight.

Summer Sun Safety

Do your little ones know that sunlight can burn our skin and that summer heat can cause dehydration? Use the action poem below to reinforce some tips on sun safety. Then, as a home-school connection, send home a copy of the note on page 9 and encourage parents to practice some summer sun safety.

When you are outside and having summer fun,   *Pretend to play or swim.*
Slop on sunscreen for protection in the sun.   *Pretend to apply sunscreen.*

Slap on a hat to give your face some shade.   *Pretend to put on a hat.*
Drink a lot of water or some frosty lemonade.   *Pretend to drink.*

Slip on a T-shirt when you're out to play.   *Pretend to put on a T-shirt.*
You don't want a sunburn to ruin your day!   *Touch skin and say "ouch!"*

Be safe this summer in the hot sunshine.   *Use hand to shade eyes.*
Slip, slap, and slop!   *Clap three times.*
And your summer will be fine.   *Nod head in agreement.*

Sing a Sunny Song

Help little ones recall what they have discovered about the sun with this lively sing-along song.

(sung to the tune of "Twinkle, Twinkle, Little Star")

The sun is big. It is so bright.
The sun shines down to give us light.
Shining down from way up high,
Shining, shining in the sky.
The sun is big. It is so bright.
The sun shines down to give us light.

The sun is hot. It can't be beat!
The sun shines down to give us heat.
Shining down from way up high,
Shining, shining in the sky.
The sun is hot. It can't be beat!
The sun shines down to give us heat.

Red-Hot Sun Booklets

Now that each little scientist knows so much about the sun, he'll want to create his own solar booklet! To make one booklet, duplicate pages 10, 11, and 12. Direct the child to cut out each booklet page on the bold lines; then help him sequence his pages and staple them between construction paper covers. If desired, use the child's construction paper print from "The Power of Sunlight" (page 7) as the front cover. Next, direct the child to complete each booklet page as suggested below.

Page 1: Sponge-print a big yellow sun shape on the page.
Page 2: Cut a sun shape from bright yellow paper. Glue the shape to the page.
Page 3: Color the semicircle at the top of the page with yellow crayon. Glue on yellow yarn sun rays.
Page 4: Cut a hat shape from fabric. Glue the hat on the child's head. Use a yellow crayon to draw a sun on the page. Color the face and draw hair.
Page 5: Color the circle yellow. Add sun rays with gold glitter glue.
Page 6: Draw and color a yellow sun above the clothesline. Color the clothes.

The sun is big. 1

The sun is bright. 2

The sun shines down to give us light. 3

The sun is hot. 4

It can't be beat! 5

The sun shines down to give us heat. 6

Dear Parents,

    We are learning about the sun and all of the ways it can help us or harm us. Please recite and perform the action poem below with your child to help reinforce some important sun safety tips. Thank you!

When you are outside and having summer fun,	*Pretend to play or swim.*
Slop on sunscreen for protection in the sun.	*Pretend to apply sunscreen.*
Slap on a hat to give your face some shade.	*Pretend to put on a hat.*
Drink a lot of water or some frosty lemonade.	*Pretend to drink.*
Slip on a T-shirt when you're out to play.	*Pretend to put on a T-shirt.*
You don't want a sunburn to ruin your day!	*Touch skin and say "ouch!"*
Be safe this summer in the hot sunshine.	*Use hand to shade eyes.*
Slip, slap, and **slop!**	*Clap three times.*
And your summer will be fine.	*Nod head in agreement.*

Booklet Pages 1 and 2
Use with "Red-Hot Sun Booklets" on page 8.

The sun is big.

1

The sun is bright.

2

The sun shines down to give us light.

3

The sun is hot.

4

It can't be beat!

5

The sun shines down to give us heat.

6

Garden Goodies

Sow the seeds of science exploration with this crop of fresh activities. Your little gardeners are sure to harvest lots of learning!

Garden Treats We Can Eat

Cucumbers, tomatoes, carrots, potatoes…the list of yummy vegetables grown in a garden seems endless! Find out which vegetables your little ones have tasted; then do a little reading to introduce them to additional veggie varieties. First, ask students to brainstorm a list of vegetables they have actually eaten as you record them on a sheet of chart paper. Then read aloud *Growing Vegetable Soup* by Lois Ehlert (Harcourt Brace & Company). Read it a second time, including the vegetable names in small print. When a vegetable from your students' list appears in the story, check it off the list. And as other vegetables are mentioned, add them to the list. Wow—vegetable goodies galore!

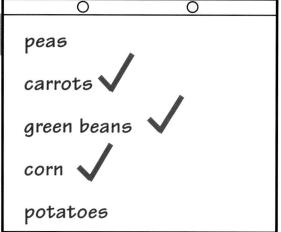

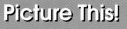

Picture This!

Now that they've made a list of vegetables, invite youngsters to search through seed catalogs to find pictures of these garden goodies. Ask children to cut out as many vegetable pictures as they like; then help them sort the pictures into labeled boxes or baskets. Next, ask small groups of students to make mini posters by gluing all the pictures of a particular vegetable to the top half of a sheet of construction paper. Display all the mini posters on a bulletin board. Then point to each poster and ask youngsters if they can name the vegetable shown. Provide the names of any unfamiliar vegetables. Print each veggie's name in large letters below the pictures. Keep the posters on display throughout your unit and refer to them for "What Can We Grow?" on page 14 and "Hey! There's a Flower in My Salad!" on page 17.

zucchini

What Can We Grow?

Reinforce the vegetable vocabulary your youngsters have learned with this simple song.

(sung to the tune of "The Wheels on the Bus")

What can we grow in the garden to eat,
Garden to eat, garden to eat?
What can we grow in the garden to eat?
We can grow [carrots].

Encourage little ones to refer to their veggie posters (see "Picture This!" on page 13) to think of other vegetable names to substitute in the last line of the song. If desired, add an additional verse describing each named vegetable:

[Carrots are orange] and good to eat,
Good to eat, good to eat.
[Carrots are orange] and good to eat.
We like [carrots]!

A Garden Graph

Mmmm…so many tasty vegetables! Which are your students' favorites? Find out when you create this graph that resembles a well-tended garden. Ask each child to pick her favorite veggie—the one she'd like to grow in an imaginary garden. Have her draw a picture of it on a quarter sheet of white construction paper. (Have younger students cut and glue pictures from magazines or seed catalogs.) Arrange the students' veggies on a bulletin board covered with brown background paper so that each veggie variety has its own row, complete with a labeled garden marker. When all the pictures are in place, read the resulting graph and discuss what it reveals.

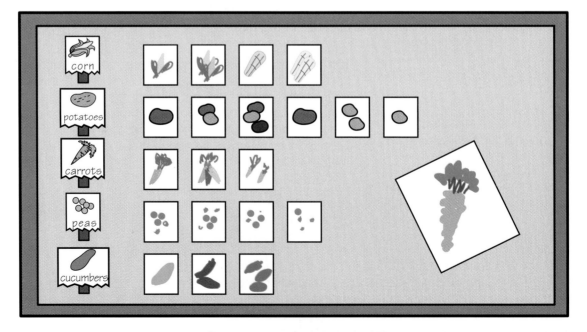

How Does Your Garden Grow?

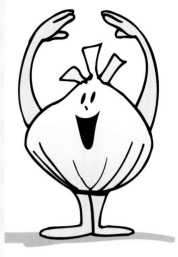

If they're going to plant any *real* vegetables, your young scientists must learn what it takes to make a plant grow. Seat youngsters in a circle and teach them this action poem to help them remember the basics.

I want to plant a vegetable here	*Point to floor.*
And watch it grow and grow.	*Move finger up until pointing at ceiling.*
I will need some good, warm soil,	*Pretend to dig with shovel.*
For plants start down below.	*Point at floor.*
And I'll need a vegetable seed	*Pretend to hold seed between thumb and forefinger.*
To put into the ground.	*Pretend to put seed into the ground.*
I'll need to give it water	*Pretend to water with watering can.*
And wet it all around.	
I'll also need the sun to shine.	*Place arms overhead to form a circle.*
That's true, without a doubt!	*Nod head.*
Soil, water, and warm sun	*Hold up one, then two, then three fingers.*
Will soon make my seed SPROUT!	*Jump up into standing position.*

Dig In!

Little imaginations will grow right along with the imaginary veggies in this sand table garden. Fill your sand table with sterilized potting soil from your local garden center or home improvement store. Provide small shovels and garden rakes, plastic flowerpots of different sizes, and large beads to represent seeds. Add some plastic vegetables from your housekeeping center. Then watch as your young gardeners get growin'!

Growing the Real Thing

With all your students now know about vegetables, the time is "ripe" for them to plant some! To prepare, punch a few holes in the bottom of a Styrofoam® cup for each child. Purchase a package or two of early-maturing radish seeds, some aquarium gravel, and some potting soil. Bring in a bunch of radishes from your grocery store. Pass the bunch around, and invite youngsters to examine it. Explain that they'll be planting some radishes and that this is what the full-grown vegetable looks like.

Working with one small group at a time, have each youngster plant a seed by following the directions below.

1. Put a layer of gravel in the bottom of a personalized cup; then fill the cup with potting soil to one-half inch below the rim.
2. Dig a shallow hole in the soil, place three radish seeds in the hole, and then cover the hole with soil.
3. Use a spray bottle of water to wet the soil until it's damp.
4. Place a plastic sandwich bag over the cup to create a warm environment for the seeds.

Once the seeds have sprouted and each little seedling has four leaves, remove all but one plant from each child's cup. Then encourage your little ones to tend to their radish plants as they continue to grow.

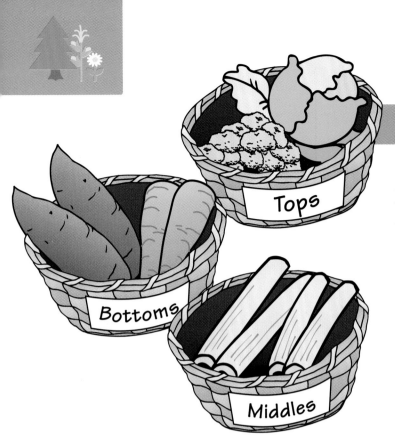

Tops, Bottoms, and In-Betweens

The hare in Janet Stevens' *Tops and Bottoms* (Harcourt Brace & Company) grows radishes and a whole lot more! Share this book with your youngsters to introduce the idea that plants have special edible parts. After reading the book, bring out real examples of the vegetables from the story. Show each vegetable to your students. Can they tell just by looking at it which part of the plant it is? Help youngsters sort the vegetables into three baskets labeled "Tops," "Bottoms," and "Middles." Mmmm...who would have guessed that plant parts could be so palatable?

Plant Parts Exploration

Leaves, roots, stems, flowers, and fruits— these are the tasty parts of plants we eat. Work with small groups of students to classify the vegetables used in "Tops, Bottoms, and In-Betweens" into these more specific categories. Pass around each vegetable and ask students if the food looks like the leaves of a plant, a cluster of flowers, an underground root, a long sturdy stem, or a part that might contain seeds (fruit). Sort the veggies into groups. Which group contains the veggies the group likes best?

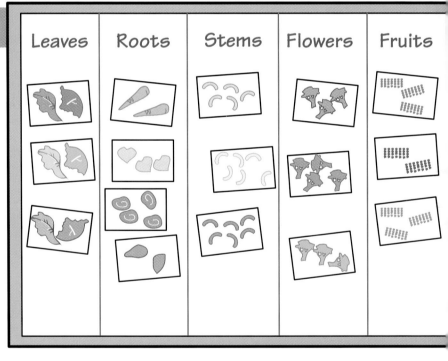

Leaves: lettuce
Roots: carrot, radish, beet
Stems: celery
Flowers: broccoli
Fruits: corn on the cob

After all your small groups have examined and categorized the vegetables, follow up with an old favorite— vegetable prints! Cut the vegetables as necessary and allow them to dry slightly. Set out shallow trays of tempera paint in a variety of colors. Encourage youngsters at your art center to dip a cut vegetable into paint and then make prints on a half sheet of white construction paper (one veggie per piece). Display the prints on a bulletin board divided into five sections, one labeled for each plant part.

Did You Know?

The fleshy part of a plant that contains the seeds is called the *fruit*. In many plants this part of the plant is sweet-tasting, which is why we typically think of apples, bananas, or melons as fruit. But some nonsweet foods we think of as *vegetables*—such as corn, peppers, tomatoes, and zucchini—are actually the fruits of their respective plants.

Hey! There's a Flower in My Salad!

A salad of leaves, roots, stems, flowers, and fruits? Sure! Bring out a basket of vegetables and explain to your youngsters that they'll be using plants with different edible parts to make a crisp and yummy Plant Parts Salad. Ask your garden detectives to identify each vegetable and to try to guess which part of the plant it represents. Show them some celery stalks (stems), a head of iceberg lettuce (leaves), a carrot or two (roots), a bunch of broccoli (flowers), and a small zucchini (fruit). Once they've identified the plant parts, have them help you wash and prepare the vegetables; then toss everything in a big salad bowl. Give each child a plastic fork, a serving of salad in a disposable bowl, and her choice of salad dressing. While they're crunching on this oh-so-healthy garden treat, ask your students to look again at the mini posters they made for "Picture This!" on page 13. Can they name some other veggies that are leaves? How about stems, flowers, roots, or fruits?

A Salad Song

Teach little ones this tune to review their salad recipe and the plant parts of each of its ingredients.

(sung to the tune of "The Hokey-Pokey")

You put some [lettuce] in
To give the salad crunch.
The [lettuce] is a [leaf]
And it's oh-so-good to munch!
You make a Plant Parts Salad
And you make it taste just right.
You'll wanna take a bite! (CRUNCH!)

Repeat the verse, substituting the other salad ingredients and corresponding plant parts for the underlined words:
carrot—root
celery—stem
zucchini—fruit
broccoli—flower

Pages and Pages of Produce

Top off your crop of vegetable investigations with this booklet featuring the best parts of plants! To prepare, photocopy pages 18–20 for each child. Have each child cut out the cover and pages for her booklet; then help her stack them and staple the booklet along the left side. Provide vegetable stickers or stamps for youngsters to use as they decorate their booklet covers. Have youngsters cut pictures of appropriate vegetables from cooking magazines or seed catalogs to glue onto each page. Encourage little ones to take their finished booklets home so they can show off their vegetable knowledge for their families.

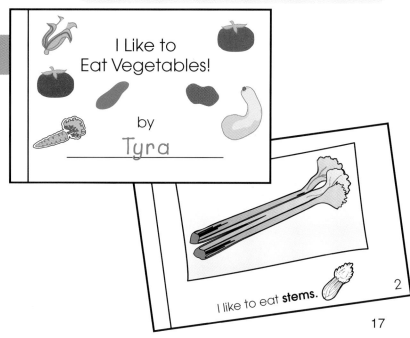

I Like to Eat Vegetables!

by

Tyra

I like to eat **stems**.

2

I Like to
Eat Vegetables!

by

_____

I like to eat **leaves.**

1

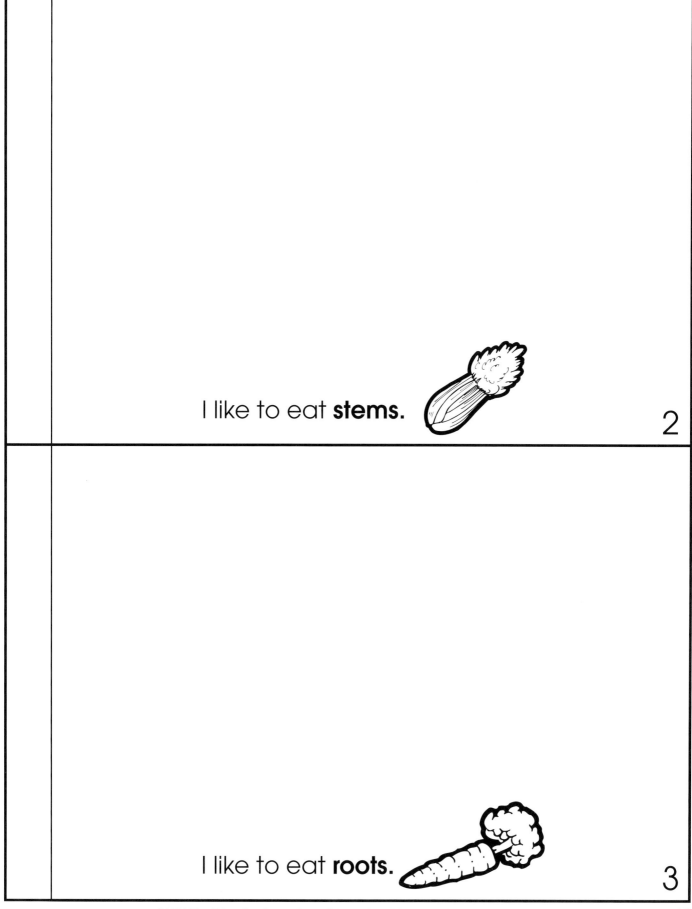

I like to eat **stems.**

2

I like to eat **roots.**

3

I like to eat **fruits.**

4

I like to eat **flowers.**

5

Cool Cuisine

When temperatures climb at the height of summer, try these refreshing activities to teach your students about some very cool foods!

Summer Foods

Ice cream, a Popsicle®, lemonade…what chilly treats do your students like to eat during the summer? Breeze into your cool cuisine theme by teaching students this short rhyme and inviting them to name their favorite summer foods.

What kind of food do you like to eat
On a hot, hot summer day?
What kind of food do you like to eat?
Tell me, [child's name], what do you say?

Jot the children's responses on a sheet of chart paper. Review the complete list; then have youngsters identify each food as hot or cold. Put a red check next to foods that are served hot or warm and a blue check next to foods served cool or frozen. How many hot foods were named? How many cold foods? Lead students to conclude that cold foods are very refreshing during hot summer months.

Favorite Summer Foods

ice cream ✔   juice ✔
lemonade ✔   watermelon ✔
hot dog ✔   soda ✔
milkshake ✔
Popsicle ✔
frozen yogurt ✔
spaghetti ✔

Our Favorite Frosty Foods

Amy likes to drink juice

...oore's Class

A Book of Frosty Foods

Extend your look at cool cuisine by making this class book. Duplicate page 26 for each child. Then invite her to add wiggle eyes and complete the facial features to create a self-portrait. Have her cut out a picture of a favorite cold food or drink from a magazine and then glue it inside the thought bubble. Have each child write her name on the first blank and write or dictate her food or drink choice on the second blank. Bind the finished pages together between white construction paper covers. Draw a few lines on the book's cover to make it resemble the front of a refrigerator. Add the title "Our Favorite Frosty Foods" and share the book during a group time. Then place the book in your reading center for further enjoyment.

Monday-to-Friday Science

Lots of foods taste great because they are chilled, but there's another reason to use a refrigerator. Here's a Monday-to-Friday project that will demonstrate why some foods *need* refrigeration. On Monday, peel a cucumber; then cut it in half. Place each cucumber half in a separate foil pan. Pass the pans around, allowing students to observe the two halves. Then loosely cover each pan with foil. Place one pan in the refrigerator. Put the other in a lidded box and place the box in a sunny spot. Leave the pans alone until Friday. On Friday, have your young scientists check both pans. They'll discover that *mold*—a tiny life form—has begun to grow on the unrefrigerated cucumber half. The refrigerated cucumber half will still look fresh.

This Is Why

Mold grew on the unrefrigerated cucumber half because it was placed in a warm location. Mold grows quickly in warm temperatures. The chilled air inside the refrigerator slowed the growing ability of the mold.

This Is Why

The warmth, water, and air inside the zippered bags made the perfect environment for growing mold on the bread. The air in the freezer was too cold for mold to grow. Plus, the cold temperatures in the freezer turned the water in the bread to ice. Ice helps to preserve foods for long periods of time.

Put the Freeze on Mold

If refrigerating foods slows down the growth of mold, what will freezing do to them? Try this experiment to find out! For each child, place a slice of day-old white bread in a personalized plastic zippered bag. Then place another slice of the bread in another zippered bag. Set out a shallow container of water and a few eyedroppers on a table. Invite each child to place a few drops of water on her bread slice before sealing the bread inside her bag. Place all these bags in a lidded box and put the box in a warm, sunny spot. Then have a student volunteer put a few drops of water on the other slice of bread. Seal it inside the zippered bag and place it in the freezer.

Encourage youngsters to check their bags daily to observe any changes. In four to seven days, your little ones will discover mold growing on the bread slices stored in the box. After two weeks, you'll have quite a collection of bread mold. Put science on display by hanging the bags from a clothesline so your students can get a really good look! Check the frozen bread periodically, too. Students will find that it has no mold at all, even after many weeks.

Cool Changes

Besides chilling foods and slowing the growth of mold, the cool temperatures of a refrigerator can do other neat things! Explore the science behind gelatin making with this delicious activity. In advance, prepare a snack of flavored gelatin for each child; set the snacks aside to be eaten later. Then invite youngsters to help you mix two same-flavored packages of gelatin—in two separate bowls—following the directions on the boxes. Encourage your little scientists to describe the color and texture of the gelatin mixtures. Then tell them that you're going to place one bowl of gelatin in the refrigerator and leave the other on a table in your room. Ask them to predict what will happen to each bowl of gelatin. Record their predictions on chart paper before putting one bowl in the refrigerator. Once it has set, place the two bowls side by side and ask youngsters to compare them. Allow them to touch the gelatin in each bowl to feel its texture and temperature. Spoon some from each bowl into a cup as youngsters observe. Lead students to conclude that chilling the gelatin changed its physical form. Finish up your activity by serving the prepared gelatin snacks. Mmm…science is delicious!

Thank You, Frank!

Did you know that the Popsicle® was invented—by accident—by eleven-year-old Frank Epperson? Frank mixed up a batch of powdered soda pop on his porch one day in the winter of 1905. But he forgot about it and left it outside overnight. The next morning, he found his pop had frozen—with the stirring stick standing straight up in it! He pulled the frozen pop from the container and the "Epperson Icicle," now known as the Popsicle, was born. Why did he change the name to Popsicle? Because the first one was created from soda *pop,* of course! Celebrate Frank Epperson's accidental invention by making these cool and fruity ice pops.

When you're ready to eat the pops, remove them from the freezer and allow them to sit for a few minutes. Then demonstrate for students how to grasp the stick and pull an ice pop out of a cup. While youngsters are slurping their frozen treats, ask them to brainstorm why cold foods cool the inside of our bodies when it's still hot outside.

Ingredients:
one 6-oz. package orange-flavored gelatin
2 c. boiling water
2 c. orange-pineapple juice

Dissolve the gelatin in the boiling water. Add the juice. Pour the mixture into three-ounce paper cups and freeze for one hour. Remove the cups from the freezer; insert a craft stick into each one. Then freeze overnight.

This Is Why

Your body has different temperature sensors. Those in your skin detect the temperature of your skin and the outside surroundings—the peripheral temperature. Other sensors inside your body detect your inside body temperature—the core temperature. So it's possible to make the inside of your body feel a bit cooler, even when the temperatures outside are high.

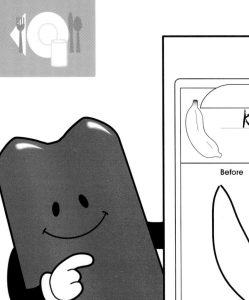

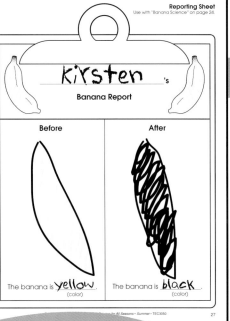

Kirsten 's

Banana Report

Before	After

The banana is **yellow**.
(color)

The banana is **black**.
(color)

©The Education Center, Inc. • Investigations for All Seasons • Summer • TEC3050   27

Banana Science

Your youngsters now know that refrigerating foods can preserve them and change their form. But the refrigerator might not be the best place to store *every* food. Try this over-the-weekend activity to find out why! In advance, purchase one banana for every two students, plus an extra one. Then duplicate the reporting sheet on page 27 to make a class supply. On a Friday, show an unpeeled banana to your group. Discuss the color and texture of the peel; then have each child draw a picture of the banana in the "before" section of her reporting sheet. Have her write the color of the fruit in the space provided. Then tell students that you're going to save the banana until Monday in the refrigerator to see if it stays fresh.

On Monday, remove the banana from the refrigerator. Have students discuss the banana's appearance and draw the banana in the "after" section of their reporting sheets. Have them write the new color in the space provided. Explain what happened to the banana (see "This Is Why") and then offer each child half of an unrefrigerated banana. Mmm…this snack is better at room temperature!

This Is Why

A banana will darken quickly in the refrigerator because the chilly temperatures produce a chemical reaction in the banana's peel. And a black banana doesn't look very appetizing! But even if you leave a banana at room temperature, it will darken—and finally turn black—because it contains a ripening hormone called *ethylene* that just doesn't know when to quit working.

Here's the Scientific Scoop

Find out more about cooling off with this delicious *and* scientific activity. In advance, purchase a class supply of ice-cream cones and enough ice cream to serve one scoop to each child. Begin the activity by asking students if their tongues feel warm or cold. Explain that the heat of our bodies makes our tongues feel warm. Then serve up the ice-cream cones and invite youngsters to slowly lick their ice cream. Ask again about the temperature of their tongues. Now they feel cold! As they continue to savor this delicious frosty food, ask youngsters to observe what is happening to the ice cream. Discuss students' observations; then explain that the heat from their tongues is traveling to the cold ice cream, warming it until it melts.

This Is Why

When you eat ice cream, heat from your tongue flows to the ice cream, warming it until it melts. As the heat travels to the ice cream, your tongue feels colder. This movement of heat is called *heat transfer*.

Think and Drink

One of the *coolest* treats on a hot summer day is a glass of refreshing water! Here's an action poem to help your little ones remember that water is the best—and healthiest—thirst quencher of all.

When it's hot, hot, hot, Fan face with hands.
I am not, not, not, Shake head "no."
Even though I run and play. Jog around in a circle.
I just think, think, think Tap forefinger on temple.
And then drink, drink, drink! Pretend to drink from a glass.
Drinking water keeps me cool all day! Wipe back of hand across forehead.

Dear Family:

At school, we're learning that drinking water is important for good health. Children can get water from good foods like fruits and vegetables and from other healthy drinks, such as milk and fruit juice. But it's also a good idea to drink some plain water every day, especially when it's hot or when exercising.

This weekend, please help your child keep track of how many glasses of plain water he or she drinks. Just have your child color in a glass for each glass of water drunk. (It isn't necessary for your child to drink all five glasses each day.) Then send this sheet back to school on Monday. Thanks for your help!

Name _____

Saturday	Sunday
1 2	1 2
3	3
4 5	4 5

©2000 The Education Center, Inc. • Science for All Seasons • Summer • TEC3086

Wet and Wonderful Water

If your youngsters work up a thirst acting out the poem in "Think and Drink," pour them cups of cold water to drink. Then share these cool facts about water while they're sipping away.

- Water accounts for more than half a human's body weight.
- Water escapes from your body easily—when you sweat, cry, go to the bathroom, and even breathe!
- As water leaves your body, it carries out wastes and cools you down.
- Drinking water replenishes your body's cooling system.
- It's especially important to drink water when the weather is hot and humid and when you are exercising a lot because you lose water through sweat.

Home Learning Lab

Include children's families in some of the cool scientific fun with this take-home weekend activity. Photocopy page 28 for each child; then send the sheets home on a Friday afternoon. When youngsters return their sheets on the following Monday, discuss the results. If desired, create a graph showing how many glasses of water were drunk on Saturday, on Sunday, or over the entire weekend.

Class Book Page

Use with "A Book of Frosty Foods" on page 21.

_____ likes _____.

_____'s

Banana Report

Before	After

The banana is _____.
(color)

The banana is _____.
(color)

Note to teacher: Use with "Banana Science" on page 24.

Dear Family:

At school, we're learning that drinking water is important for good health. Children can get water from good foods like fruits and vegetables and from other healthy drinks, such as milk and fruit juice. But it's also a good idea to drink some plain water every day, especially when it's hot or when exercising.

This weekend, please help your child keep track of how many glasses of plain water he or she drinks. Just have your child color in a glass for each glass of water drunk. (It isn't necessary for your child to drink all five glasses each day.) Then send this sheet back to school on Monday. Thanks for your help!

Name _____

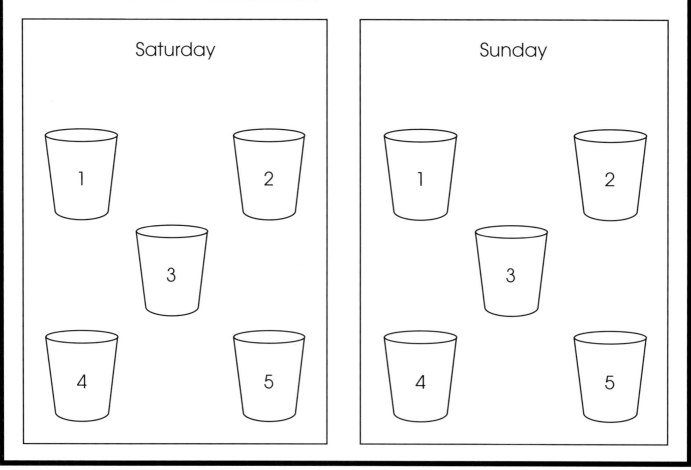

©2000 The Education Center, Inc. • *Science for All Seasons* • *Summer* • TEC3050

28   **Note to the teacher:** Use with "Home Learning Lab" on page 25.

Science in the Sandbox

Involve your youngsters in lots of discovery learning
with this sensational selection of sand-based explorations.

Sandbox Site Setup

A sandy exploration site is a must for the activities in this unit! If you do not have a sand table in your classroom, substitute a large shallow plastic tub with a lid. Half-fill the tub with sandbox sand (available by the bag at home improvement stores). This versatile container can be used on tables, on the floor, or outdoors. When it is time for the beach to close, merely snap on the lid for easy storage.

Sandbags

Introduce your youngsters to the wonder of sand with this simple observation activity. To prepare, pour one-half cup of sand in a plastic resealable bag for each child. Secure each bag by placing a strip of masking tape over the sealed end. Then ask each child to observe the sand in his bag using a magnifying glass. Encourage your students to describe the color, shape, and size of the sand grains. Then have each child explore further by squeezing, shaking, and turning his bag of sand upside down for a closer look. How observant!

Sand Discovery Tools

Need a supply of inexpensive tools for your sand site? Use this idea to make funnels and sand scoops from plastic containers. In advance, collect a variety of clean, empty plastic bottles and jugs. To make a funnel, cut off the bottom half of a plastic bottle and remove the cap. To make a sand scoop, cut off the bottom of a plastic milk jug as shown. (Be sure to cover any sharp edges with masking tape.) Place these tools at your sand site. Add a variety of traditional sand pails and shovels; then let your little ones dig in!

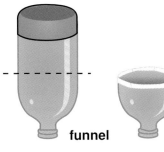

funnel

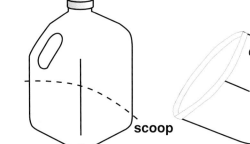

scoop

Sensory Sand

Get your youngsters in touch with sand explorations using this hands-on activity and song. To begin, invite a small group of students to the sand table. Then sing the song below as they perform the corresponding actions. Afterward, discuss students' sand explorations and invite them to describe their experiences.

Sandy Action Song
(sung to the tune of "London Bridge")

Put your hands down in the sand,
In the sand, in the sand.
Put your hands down in the sand
To explore it!

Let the sand spill from your hands,
From your hands, from your hands.
Let the sand spill from your hands
To explore it!

Build a pile with the sand,
With the sand, with the sand.
Build a pile with the sand
To explore it!

Dig a deep hole in the sand,
In the sand, in the sand.
Dig a deep hole in the sand
To explore it!

Pouring and More

This sand investigation is overflowing with learning possibilities! In advance, collect several different-sized funnels, a small plastic pail, and a watch with a second hand. Gather your students around the sand table and have them observe the sand as you pour it through each funnel. Encourage them to compare the sand flowing out of the different funnels. Next, pour the sand through the smallest funnel and fill the pail. Use the watch to time how long it takes to fill the pail; then record the results on a sheet of chart paper. Use the remaining funnels, in turn, to fill the pail. Record the different times on the chart and then discuss the results. Lead students to conclude that the larger funnels filled the pail faster because the sand flowed through the funnels faster.

A Cup Full of Sand

Invite your youngsters to further their sand studies with this prediction and measurement activity. In advance, collect four clean, empty plastic containers in a variety of sizes. Label each container with a different number from one to four. Then place the containers at the sand table along with a one-cup plastic measuring cup. Invite a small group of students to join you at the sand table. Show them the measuring cup and the first container; then have each child predict the number of cups it will take to fill the container. Next, invite students to count aloud as you pour each cup of sand into the container. When the container is filled, compare students' predictions with the actual number needed. Continue the prediction and measuring process until each container has been filled. When each small group has completed this activity, use the idea below to have students record their sand-filled findings.

Gritty Graph

Use this graphing idea to help students record their discoveries from "A Cup Full of Sand" (above). To prepare, make a copy of page 34 for each child. Place the four plastic containers (from "A Cup Full of Sand") in a row on a table. To begin, hold up the first container and ask students to recall how many cups of sand it took to fill the container. Then have each child color her graph accordingly. Continue this activity in the same manner with the remaining three containers. If youngsters are unsure of the number of cups needed to fill a specific container, have a volunteer return to the sand table to measure it. Now that's a task that's filled to the brim with science!

Just Add Water!

Introduce your youngsters to the wonders of wet sand with this demonstration. First, invite a small group of students to join you at the sand table. Ask them to observe as you heap sand into a small pile, then dig a shallow hole in the top of it. Next, slowly pour in one-half cup of water. Encourage your students to describe how the sand changes with the addition of water. Then record their responses on a sheet of chart paper to use with "Sand Packin' " (below).

Sand Packin'

Pack more learning into your sand site with this comparison experiment. To prepare, fill a bucket with dry sand and set it aside. Then add enough water to your sand table until the sand clumps and is just right for molding into shapes. Invite a small group of students to the sand table. Review the chart from "Just Add Water!" and briefly discuss how sand changes with the addition of water. Next, give each child a plastic cup and spoon. Have him use his spoon to pack his cup with wet sand. Next, show your youngsters how to gently turn the cup over and remove it to reveal a mini sand castle. Then ask each child to fill his cup with dry sand, and gently turn it over next to his wet sand shape. Encourage students to compare the appearance of the wet and dry sand shapes. Then lead them to conclude that wet sand "sticks" together much better than dry sand. What a heap of fun!

Soggy Sand

Your little ones know that adding water to sand can make it stick together, but do they know what will happen if too much water is added? Use this activity to find out! To prepare, provide each child with a cup of water, a plastic spoon, and a plastic bowl containing one-half cup of sand. Direct each child to slowly add water to his bowl, one spoonful at a time, until the dry sand becomes wet enough to shape into a pile. Next, have students predict what will happen if more water is added to the sand pile. Then ask each child to add more water to his bowl until the sand is runny. Discuss your students' observations. As an extension, have youngsters brainstorm ways to remove the water from the sand, such as using a filter or setting the sand in the sun. That's making the best out of a sticky situation!

This Is Why

Sand is made up of many tiny individual grains. Dry grains of sand can be heaped together, but they won't stick together. When water is added to sand, each grain becomes surrounded by a little bit of the liquid. The *surface tension* created by the water around the grains of sand causes them to stick or clump together.

Sandy Structures

Challenge your little sand sculptors to use their experience with molding wet sand to build a castle. Provide your building team with buckets, cups, and other different-shaped containers to use as molds for the wet sand at the site. Then let the packing, molding, and building begin. When your students have completed their castle, take a picture of it to document the project. Encourage your youngsters to inspect the structure each morning for any observable changes as the sand dries out. Snap a photo of the structure to document the changes. Later have your students sequence the photographs to show the progression of change in the "sand-tastic" castle.

What Can I Do With Sand?

Top off your students' scientific sand studies with this unique booklet. To prepare, duplicate pages 35, 36, and 37 for each child. Direct her to cut out the pages along the bold lines and then complete each page as suggested below. Next, help the child sequence her pages, stack them in order, and staple them together along the top. Have each child store her booklet in a plastic resealable bag; then encourage her to take the sand-embellished booklet home to share with her family.

Cover: Write your name on the line. Lay the cover over a piece of sandpaper and rub a crayon over it to make a sandlike texture.

Page 1: Color the bucket. Glue sand in the bucket to look like it is piled up.

Page 2: Color the scoop. Glue sand on to look like it is pouring out of the scoop.

Page 3: Glue sand inside each cup shape.

Page 4: Glue sand inside the sandbox. Glue on a catalog picture of a sand toy.

Page 5: Draw a picture to show something else you can do with sand. Glue sand to your drawing.

What Can I Do With Sand?
by Lucic

I can pile it. 1

I can pour it. 2

1.
2.
I can pack it.

I can play with it. 4

What else can I do with sand? 5

33

Name _____

Cups of Sand

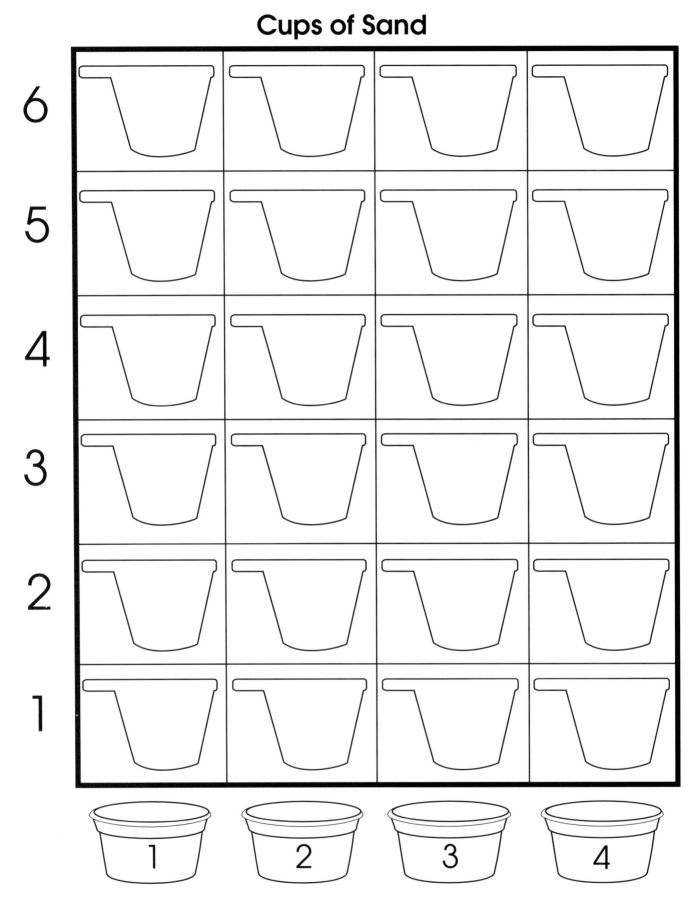

Note to the teacher: Use with "Gritty Graph" on page 31.

1

I can pile it.

What Can I Do With Sand?

by _____

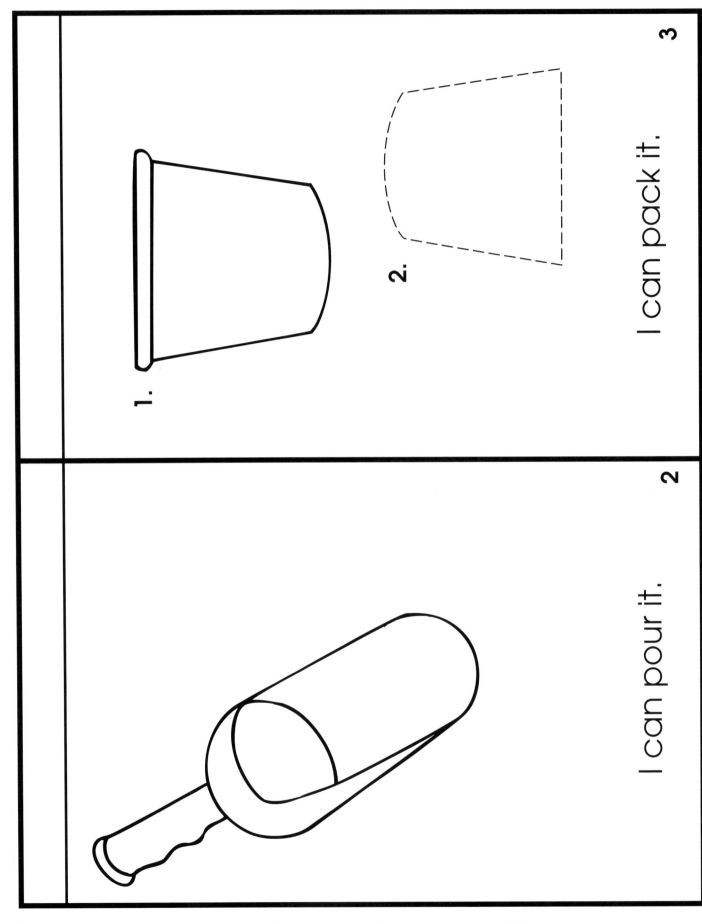

3

I can pack it.

1.

2.

2

I can pour it.

5

What else can I
do with sand?

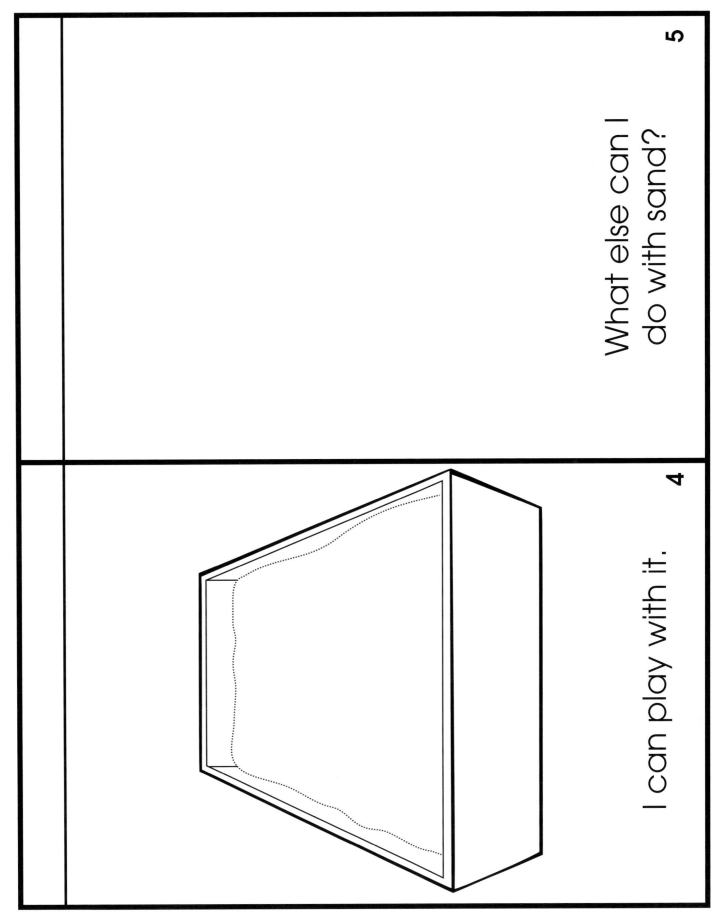

4

I can play with it.

Seesaws, Swings, and Playground Things

Seesaws and swings are scientific? Absolutely! Use the ideas in this unit to teach your youngsters about some simple machines and other physics concepts. You won't have to go any farther than the most popular place in school—the playground!

Playing Favorites

Swing right into this science study with a reading of Gail Gibbons's *Playgrounds* (Holiday House, Inc.). Which things in Gibbons's story are on your school playground? Talk about the equipment that isn't familiar to your students. Then get your little ones thinking about *their* favorite pieces of playground equipment by singing this tune.

(sung to the tune of "Paw-Paw Patch")

Do you head for the slide when you go outside?
Run to the swings, hop on the glide?
Climb up the monkey bars on the side?
What do you head for when you go outside?

Invite each child to name her favorite piece of playground equipment and tell why she likes it so much. Then go outdoors and experience the fun of the playground firsthand!

swing | slide | merry-g

Photo Graph

Which piece of playground equipment is the most popular in your classroom? Find out with this activity that helps youngsters practice their prediction, graphing, and counting skills. First, ask students to predict which piece of playground equipment is most popular, and record their responses. Then, during an outdoor playtime, photograph each child on her favorite piece of playground equipment. Ask for double prints when you have the pictures developed. (Save one set for "Playground Moves" on page 43.) Then label a graph to reflect the playground equipment chosen. Ask each youngster to place her photo on the graph in the appropriate column. Together, count the photos in each column and compare the results of the graph to your students' predictions.

The Ups and Downs of Seesaws

Playing with a pal on a seesaw is a perennial playground pleasure. Explore the seesaw's ups and downs with this small-group activity. To prepare, gather one paper towel tube for every two students in the group. Cut the tubes in half lengthwise. Also gather a ruler and a supply of wooden counting cubes for each pair.

Begin the activity by taking the group out to your playground to check out a real seesaw. Have them examine the parts of the seesaw. Move it up and down so that they can observe it working. Then go back indoors and invite youngsters to make their own miniature seesaws. Provide each pair with a paper-towel-tube half, a ruler, and some counting cubes. Demonstrate how to set the ruler on top of the tube half to resemble a seesaw. Have students make their own seesaws and experiment with placing the cubes on either end of the ruler. Can they make their seesaws balance? What happens if they change the placement of the tube half? After your student pairs have tested their tabletop seesaws, invite them back outdoors to try out their findings on a *real* seesaw!

This Is Why

A seesaw is an example of a simple machine known as a *lever.* A lever consists of a stiff bar that turns on a resting point, or *fulcrum.* If you push one end of a lever down, the other end moves up. Changing the placement of the fulcrum (in this case, the tube half) changes the weight (in this case, the number of blocks) needed to balance the two ends.

Flipped Out!

Don't put away those rulers and paper-towel-tube halves yet! Use them again to further explore levers. First, find a flat spot on your playground; it can be as small as a picnic table or as large as a blacktop area. Bring along the rulers and tube halves, as well as a cup of Cheerios® cereal (or similar cereal) and a few small clean cans (such as tuna cans). Set up a seesaw and place a can a few inches away. Remind students that when you push down on one end of a lever, the other end moves up. Then demonstrate how to place a piece of cereal on one end of a ruler and then push the opposite end down in order to flip the cereal into the air and (if you're lucky) into the can. Have students take turns flipping the cereal pieces with the mini seesaws. How many can they land in a can?

A Seesaw Song

Reinforce the movements of a seesaw with this song and its accompanying motions. Encourage youngsters to stand on tiptoe when they sing the word *up* and to squat down low when they sing the word *down*.

(sung to the tune of "Did You Ever See a Lassie?")

Have you ridden on a seesaw,
A seesaw, a seesaw?
Have you ridden on a seesaw?
It goes up and down.
When one side is up,
The other side's down.
Have you ridden on a seesaw?
It goes up and down.

Swing Set Science

Now that your class has explored the seesaw, swing on over to the swing set for more scientific fun! During a group time, ask each of your youngsters to think about sitting in a swing. Ask questions such as the following: How do you get the swing started? How do you make the swing go high? How do you make the swing stop moving?

After discussing students' ideas, go out to your swing set and give everyone a turn to swing. Ask youngsters to pay close attention to what they do with their bodies to control the movement of the swing. When you return to the classroom, paraphrase the information in "This Is Why" for your swingin' scientists!

This Is Why

A swing is actually a *pendulum*. A pendulum is an object suspended at the end of a string or wire that pivots around a fixed point. Once you start to swing, you have to move your upper body and your legs back and forth, but the movement must be done *at the right time*. To make the swing go high, you keep "pumping" and the movement of the swing gradually builds up. Small pushes at the right times cause the swing to go higher.

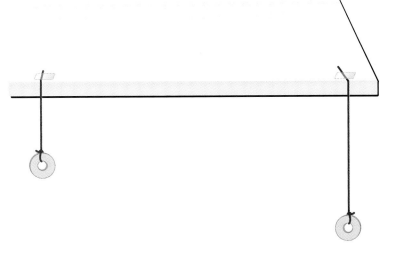

Swinging Strings

Encourage your youngsters to explore pendulums further with this simple idea for your science center. Tape several varied lengths of string to the edge of a table, spacing them about two feet apart. Tie a metal washer or a binder clip to the free end of each string. Encourage youngsters at this center to start one of the strings swinging and then count the number of times it goes back and forth before it comes to a stop. Does the length of the string affect the number of times it swings back and forth?

Let It Flow

Combine pendulums and sand play for this fascinating outdoor activity. In advance, make a few sand pendulums—enough for each child in a small group to have one. To make one, punch a penny-sized hole in the bottom of a plastic cup. Punch three holes around the rim of the cup; then thread an 18-inch length of string through each of the three holes, gather the ends, and knot them together. Take the sand pendulums, a tarp, and a small group of students out to your sandbox. If your playground does not have a sandbox, fill a large plastic tub with sand (available by the bag at home improvement stores).

Spread the tarp near the sandbox. Have each child cover the hole in the bottom of his cup with a few fingers and then fill the cup with sand. Have him hold the cup by the knotted strings and then gently push it once, letting the sand flow through the hole. (Be sure the hand holding the strings remains still.) Have him observe what happens to the sand. When the group is done watching the sandy designs made by their pendulums, gather the tarp edges and return the sand to the sandbox. If desired, create a sand pendulum with longer strings and attach it to a set of monkey bars for youngsters to use during outdoor play times.

This Is Why

Gravity and the swinging motion of the cup made the sandy design. Gravity works to pull the sand straight down to the ground, but the swinging motion of the cup causes the sand to fall in a line.

Going Up

Slide into more scientific study of your playground with this uplifting activity. In advance, gather five heavy books (such as encyclopedia volumes), a jump rope, and a canvas tote bag. Gather your youngsters near your playground slide. Place the books inside the bag; then tie one end of the jump rope to the bag handles. Place the bag of books near the slide's steps and ask your group, "What's the easiest way to get the bag of books to the top of the slide?" Discuss student responses. Then have a child stand at the top of the slide. Hand him the free end of the rope and have him try to pull the books straight up. [**Safety note:** Stand directly behind him as he attempts to pull up the books.] Next, place the bag of books at the bottom of the sliding board. Have the same child try to pull the books up the slide. Repeat this process over your next few outdoor play times, until every child has had a chance to try it. Then discuss the process. Was it easier to pull the books up the slide or directly up from the ground?

This Is Why

The sliding board is a simple machine known as an *inclined plane*. An inclined plane is a flat surface that has one end higher than the other. Inclined planes make it easier to move heavy objects from one height to another. Thus, it took less effort to pull the bag of books up the slide than it did to lift them straight up from the ground.

Going Down

Here's another activity that's just "plane" fun! Set up a ramp center by propping up one end of a flat board or a piece of sturdy cardboard on a stack of books. Bring out various sizes of toy cars and place them in a basket near the ramp. Show youngsters in a small group how to place a car at the top of the ramp and *release* (not push) it. Encourage students to pay special attention to how far the vehicle rolls after it leaves the ramp. After each child has had an opportunity to work with the ramp and cars, ask the group to predict what will happen if more books are added to make the ramp steeper. Add one book to your stack and invite youngsters to test this idea. Did any vehicles travel further from the higher ramp? Keep stacking and rolling as student interest dictates.

Slip-Slidin' Away

Which materials will help you slide down a sliding board faster? Which will slow you down? Your playground scientists will jump at the chance to find out! In advance, gather various materials to test, such as carpet squares, bath towels, bath mats, squares of burlap and other fabrics, bubble wrap, nylon jackets, raincoats, and winter coats. Display all the items and ask youngsters to predict which materials will help them go quickly down the slide. Jot students' predictions on a chart. Then pile all the materials into a box or a wagon and head outdoors to give them a try. Keep this experiment going over the course of a few outdoor play times, so that each child has a turn to test all the items. Then discuss the results. Which materials helped increase sliding speed? Which ones slowed your youngsters down?

This Is Why

Some smooth materials, such as nylon, will send you zooming quickly down the slide. Textured materials, such as burlap or a rubber-backed bath mat, will slow you down, as will materials like vinyl and leather that have a surface stickiness. To slide quickly, there needs to be a minimum of *friction,* or resistance, between the material and the slide. Textured and sticky materials create more friction on the slide's surface and make you slide more slowly.

Playground Moves

Move right into language fun when you have students create these adorable booklets! To prepare, photocopy page 44 onto colorful construction paper and page 45 onto white copy paper for each child. Read through the directions below and gather the necessary materials. Use the extra set of prints you saved from "Photo Graph" on page 38 for the final pages of the booklets. Direct each child to cut apart his cover and pages, and to cut out the patterns for the seesaw, swing, and merry-go-round. Have him cut out the slide pattern, trace it onto aluminum foil, and cut around the outline. Then have him complete his booklet as directed below. Staple each finished booklet in the upper left corner.

Cover: Write your name on the line.
Page 1: Use a brad to attach the seesaw cutout to the page where indicated.
Page 2: Glue the foil cutout onto the slide.
Page 3: Punch holes on the page where indicated. Cut two short lengths of yarn. Tape the yarn lengths to the back of the swing cutout. Thread the free ends of the yarn through the holes and tape them to the back of the page.
Page 4: Use a brad to attach the merry-go-round cutout to the page where indicated.
Page 5: Trim your photo to fit the page; then glue it in place. Write or dictate your favorite playground movement.

If You're So Inclined...

Ask your youngsters if they can think of other examples of inclined planes. Use the list below to help get them started.

a water slide	a set of stairs
a mountain	a bathtub bottom
roller coaster rails	a ramp
a ladder	a rooftop

Playground Patterns

Use with "Playground Moves" on page 43.

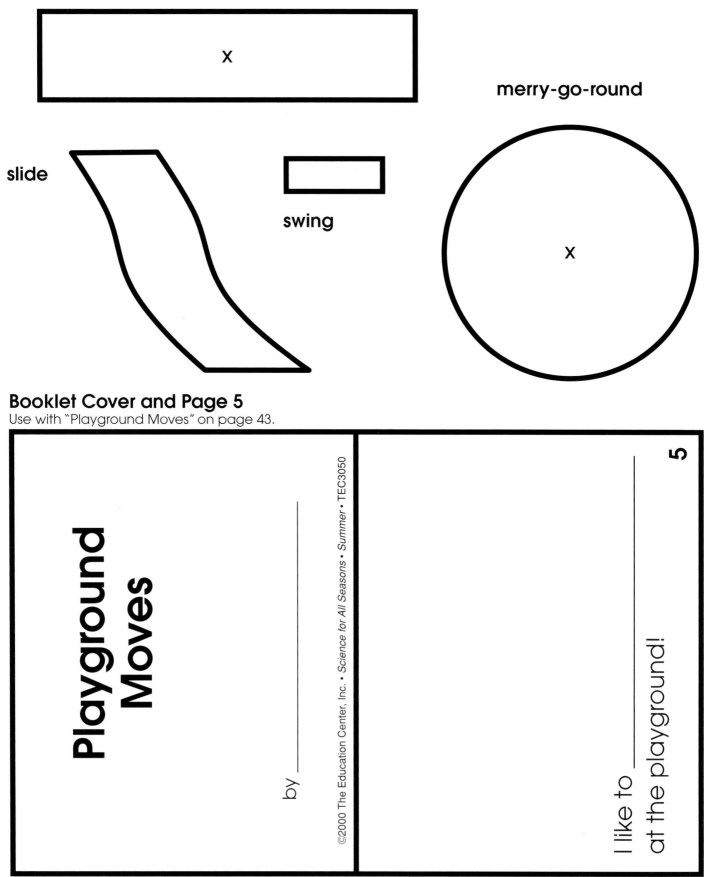

seesaw

x

merry-go-round

slide

swing

x

Booklet Cover and Page 5

Use with "Playground Moves" on page 43.

5

Playground Moves

by _____

©2000 The Education Center, Inc. • *Science for All Seasons* • *Summer* • TEC3050

I like to _____
at the playground!

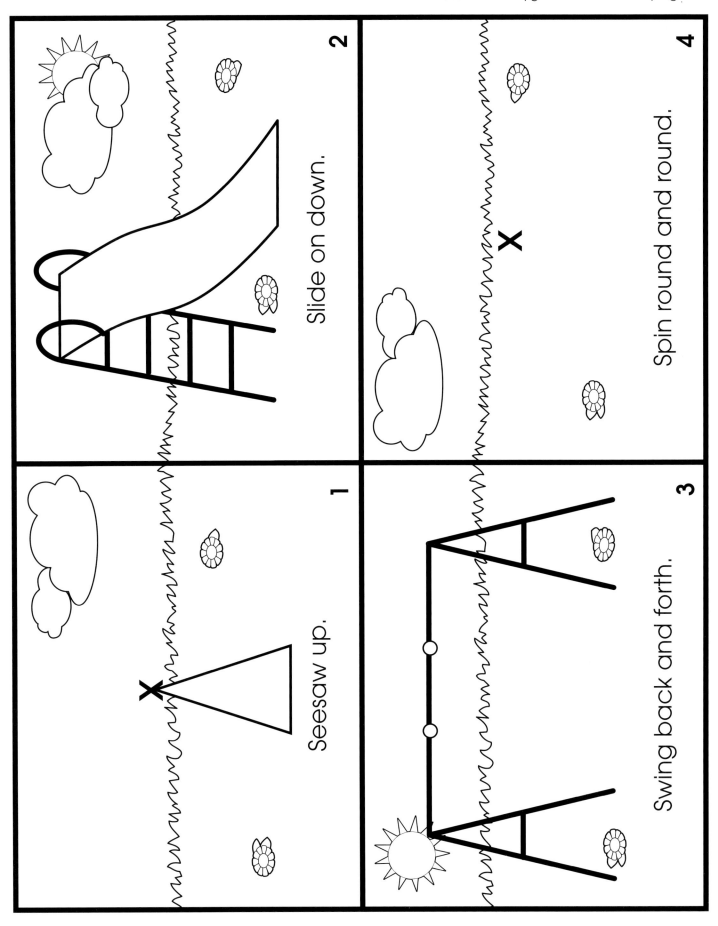

2

Slide on down.

4

Spin round and round.

X

1

Seesaw up.

X

3

Swing back and forth.

Books About Bugs

Introduce your youngsters to this collection of insect books and they will be all abuzz about bugs!

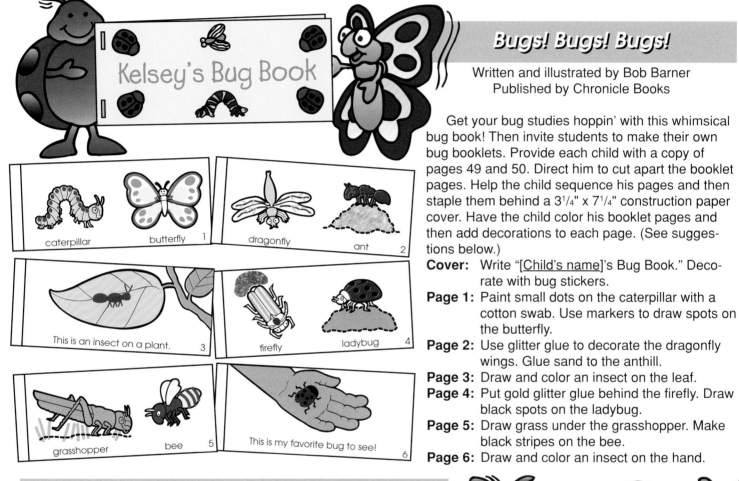

Bugs! Bugs! Bugs!

Written and illustrated by Bob Barner
Published by Chronicle Books

Get your bug studies hoppin' with this whimsical bug book! Then invite students to make their own bug booklets. Provide each child with a copy of pages 49 and 50. Direct him to cut apart the booklet pages. Help the child sequence his pages and then staple them behind a 3$\frac{1}{4}$" x 7$\frac{1}{4}$" construction paper cover. Have the child color his booklet pages and then add decorations to each page. (See suggestions below.)

Cover: Write "[Child's name]'s Bug Book." Decorate with bug stickers.
Page 1: Paint small dots on the caterpillar with a cotton swab. Use markers to draw spots on the butterfly.
Page 2: Use glitter glue to decorate the dragonfly wings. Glue sand to the anthill.
Page 3: Draw and color an insect on the leaf.
Page 4: Put gold glitter glue behind the firefly. Draw black spots on the ladybug.
Page 5: Draw grass under the grasshopper. Make black stripes on the bee.
Page 6: Draw and color an insect on the hand.

Ladybug at Orchard Avenue

Written by Kathleen Weidner Zoehfeld
Illustrated by Thomas Buchs
Published by Soundprints

Invite your youngsters to follow along as you read about a ladybug's busy day. Then teach them the poem below to reinforce the facts they've learned about this well-known bug!

A ladybug can fly up high   *Point up above head.*
And crawl on the ground so low.   *Move fingertips along floor.*
A ladybug eats aphids
Till it's very full, you know!   *Pat tummy.*
A ladybug finds a warm, dark hole *Cup left hand to make a "hole."*
And crawls deep inside to rest.   *Put right thumb into cupped hand.*
A ladybug sleeps deeply
In its little winter nest.   *Close eyes and pretend to sleep.*

Where Butterflies Grow

Written by Joanne Ryder
Illustrated by Lynne Cherry
Published by Puffin Books

Fascinate your little learners with this book about the stages of a butterfly's life. After reading the story, help students recall the different stages of a butterfly's life. (See "Butterfly Life Cycle.") Then have each child follow the directions below to create a butterfly life cycle wheel.

Butterfly Life Cycle

Egg

Caterpillar—the wormlike larvae that hatch from the butterfly egg

Pupa—the form of a butterfly while it is in the *chrysalis,* a shell-like covering

Butterfly

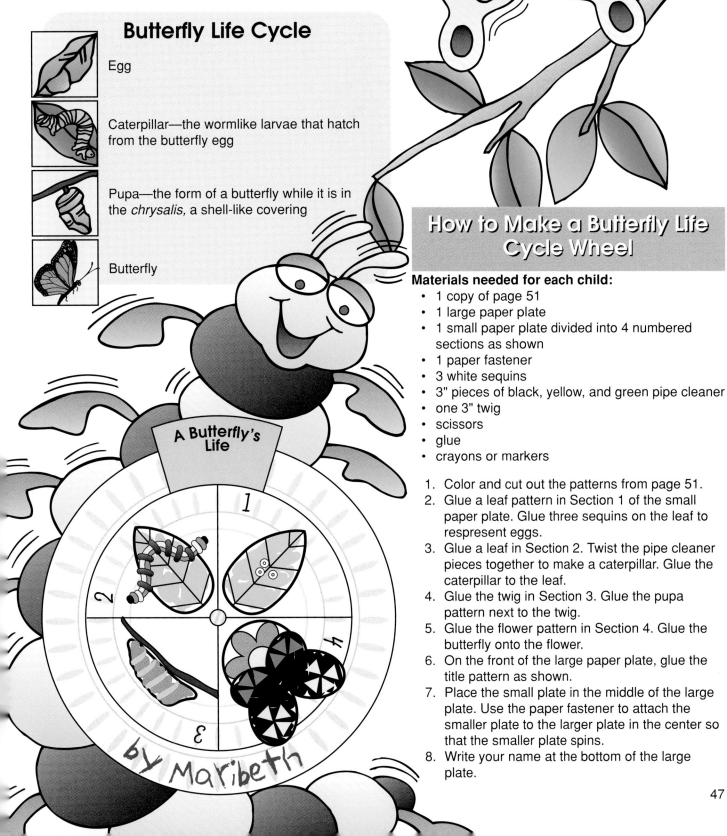

How to Make a Butterfly Life Cycle Wheel

Materials needed for each child:
* 1 copy of page 51
* 1 large paper plate
* 1 small paper plate divided into 4 numbered sections as shown
* 1 paper fastener
* 3 white sequins
* 3" pieces of black, yellow, and green pipe cleaner
* one 3" twig
* scissors
* glue
* crayons or markers

1. Color and cut out the patterns from page 51.
2. Glue a leaf pattern in Section 1 of the small paper plate. Glue three sequins on the leaf to respresent eggs.
3. Glue a leaf in Section 2. Twist the pipe cleaner pieces together to make a caterpillar. Glue the caterpillar to the leaf.
4. Glue the twig in Section 3. Glue the pupa pattern next to the twig.
5. Glue the flower pattern in Section 4. Glue the butterfly onto the flower.
6. On the front of the large paper plate, glue the title pattern as shown.
7. Place the small plate in the middle of the large plate. Use the paper fastener to attach the smaller plate to the larger plate in the center so that the smaller plate spins.
8. Write your name at the bottom of the large plate.

Oh, Doug! A Dragonfly's Day

Written by Ann Leach
Illustrated by Russell Aldredge
Published by Take Flight Publications

What's one insect that spends a lot of time hovering above the water? The dragonfly! Delight your youngsters with this book about this beautiful and interesting insect. After reading the story, provide each student with a construction paper copy of the dragonfly patterns on page 52. Help the child identify the four main body parts of a dragonfly (*head, thorax, wings,* and *abdomen*). Then have her color and cut out the patterns. Next, direct her to glue the head, thorax, and abdomen patterns to the body base pattern. Have her use glitter glue to decorate the wings and then glue them onto the thorax. Finally, direct the child to glue two large wiggle eyes to the dragonfly's head. When each child has completed a dragonfly, recite the poem below as students maneuver their dragonflies through the air.

It's a Dragonfly!

What has a body that's small in size?
What has two big enormous eyes?
What has a head, thorax, and abdomen, too?
What hovers over the pond so blue?
What catches bugs as it flies through the air?
It's a dragonfly! See it flying there?

The Honey Makers

Written and illustrated by Gail Gibbons
Published by William Morrow and Company, Inc.

This honey of a book will provide amazing facts about some of the busiest insects—bees! After reading and discussing the story, have each child make a model hive and honeybee. To make a hive, have him use a hexagon-shaped sponge to print a yellow honeycomb pattern on a piece of white paper. Set the paper aside to dry.

To make a honeybee, have a child use tacky glue to glue three one-inch yellow pom-poms together as shown. Then have him wrap a six-inch brown pipe cleaner around the third pom-pom to resemble stripes. Have the child glue features to his honeybee, such as construction paper eyes and tissue paper wings. Then have him glue the bee to his hive. Invite the child to dictate something he's learned about honeybees. Then write his response on his paper. Display these "bee-autiful" insect projects for all to see! Bzzzzz!

A honeybee makes honey.

Sam

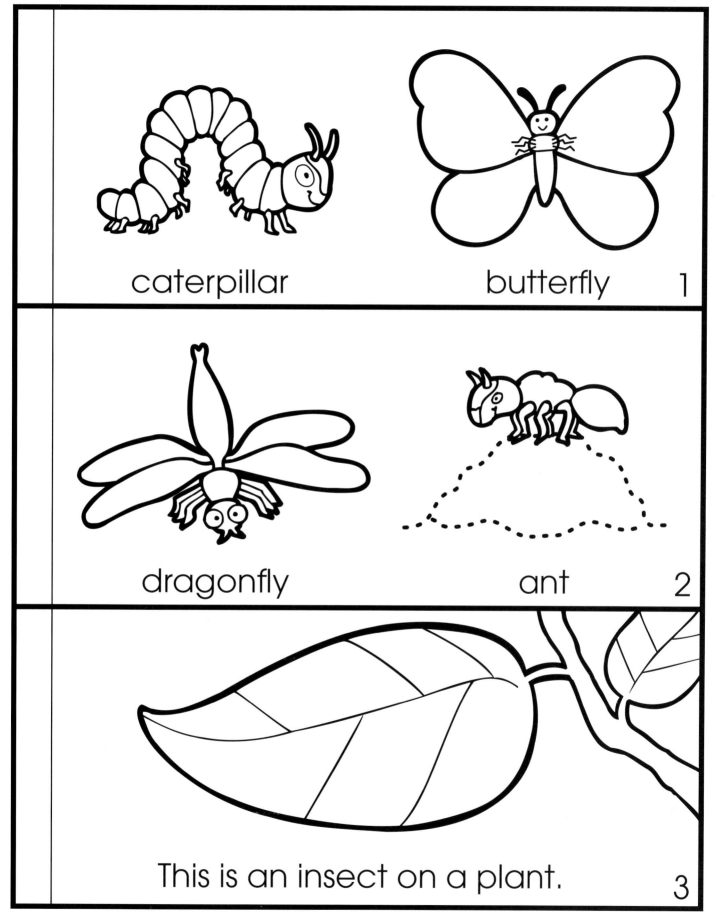

caterpillar   butterfly   1

dragonfly   ant   2

This is an insect on a plant.   3

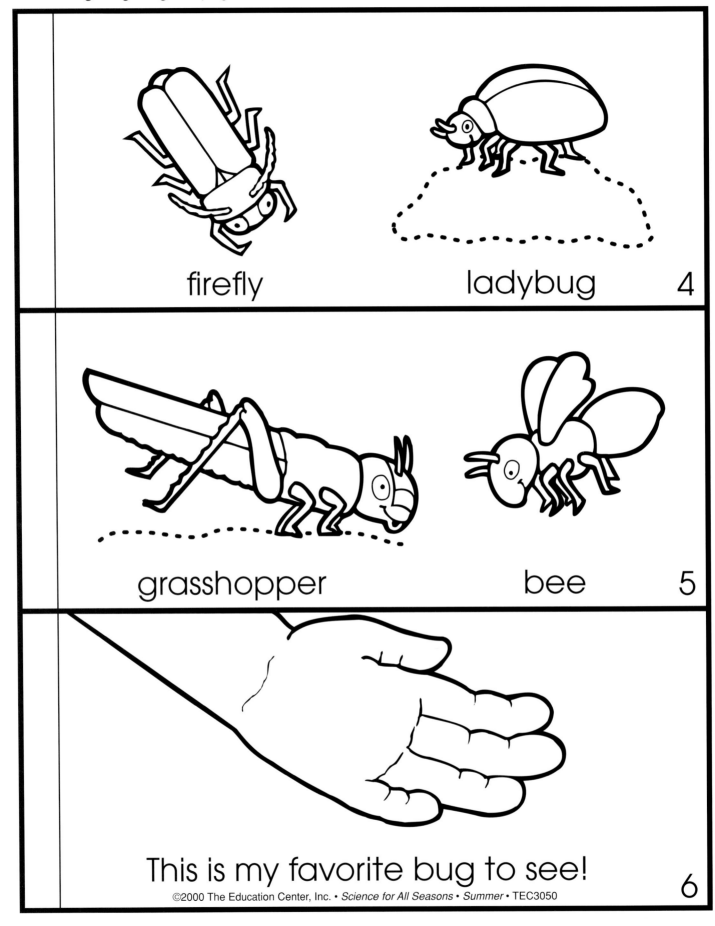

firefly   ladybug   4

grasshopper   bee   5

This is my favorite bug to see!   6

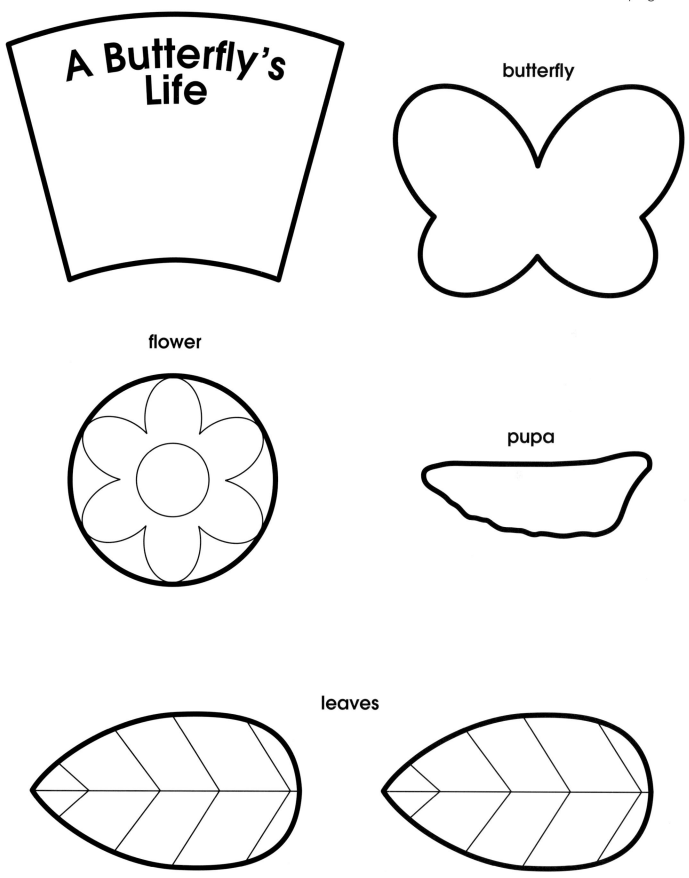

A Butterfly's Life

butterfly

flower

pupa

leaves

Dragonfly Patterns

Use with *Oh, Doug! A Dragonfly's Day* on page 48.

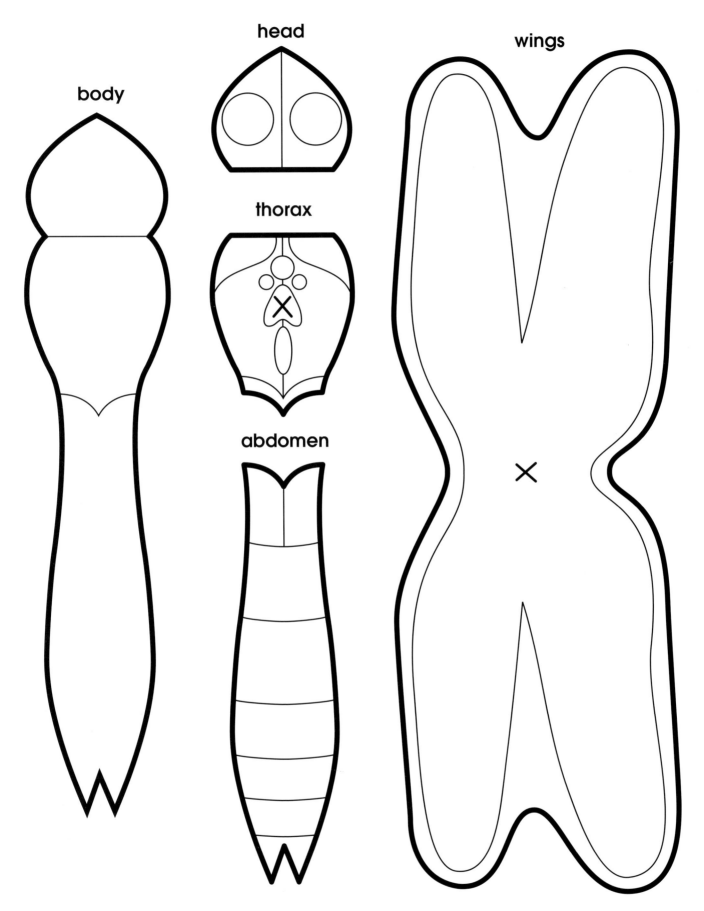

body

head

wings

thorax

abdomen

The Scientific Artist

Exploring Chalk

What would summer be like without the color and fun of chalk drawings on the sidewalk? Your little ones will be drawn to the wonders of chalk as they explore this art medium indoors and out!

Let's Talk About Chalk!

Invite your youngsters to explore the many interesting attributes of chalk with this critical-thinking activity. In advance, put a piece of chalk in a small cardboard box. Begin the activity by shaking the box and reciting the poem shown in the speech bubble. Encourage each child to guess what is in the box. Once everyone has had a turn to guess, reveal the mystery piece of chalk. Have each student examine the chalk by looking at it, touching it, and smelling it. Invite your youngsters to describe the chalk. Then record each student's description on the chalkboard or a piece of chart paper. Encourage your youngsters to suggest different uses for chalk. Are your little scientists doing some creative thinking? Chalk it up to science!

Chalk

dusty   pretty
light   small
dry   breaks easily

Something small is in this box.
What do you think it could be?
You can use it during art time
To draw a picture of me!

You can draw with it on paper
Or on a big sidewalk.
Do you know what it is?
Yes, it's a piece of...

Textured Chalk Drawings

Acquaint your little ones to the versatility of chalk by having them put this drawing tool to the test! In advance, gather a supply of each of the following materials: copier paper, black construction paper, sandpaper, foil, corrugated cardboard, and smooth cardboard. Then, for each child, cut a three-inch square from each material. Have the child glue his squares onto a large piece of construction paper. Then have him use a piece of yellow chalk to color each square. When everyone has finished, discuss how well the chalk works on each surface. Have students vote on the best surface on which to create a chalk masterpiece. You're sure to hear a lot of chatter about chalk!

Erasable Chalk?

Now that your youngsters have used chalk to color, have them discover its erasability. Direct each student to use colored chalk to draw a large circle on a piece of white paper. Then encourage her to use a cotton ball to try to erase her circle. Next, have her repeat the process using a small chalkboard (or the classroom chalkboard) and a cotton ball. After discussing the results with your class, your little ones will conclude that chalk erases better from certain surfaces!

This Is Why

A chalkboard is smooth and hard. Chalk will stay on the surface of the board, making it easy to erase. A piece of construction paper has fibers. The chalk gets caught in the fibers, making it more difficult to erase.

Outside Chalk Explorations

Involve your students in exploring the marvels of chalk…outside on a sidewalk! To prepare, gather a class supply of colored chalk, small brooms, cloth pieces, and a bucket of water. Lead your class to an area of sidewalk and instruct each student to make a chalk drawing. When each child has finished, encourage her to try to erase the drawing with a broom. Next, have her make another attempt at erasing her drawing using a piece of cloth. Then have the student wet her piece of cloth in the bucket of water and try erasing her artwork. Discuss the results and ask students if they can think of an even better way to erase chalk from a sidewalk *(a bucketful of water or water from a hose)*. Invite students to create more chalk drawings and then use the method they like best to erase them!

C-H-A-L-K!

Use this catchy tune to reinforce what students have already learned about chalk. After singing the verse below, extend the song by using student suggestions in place of the underlined word. C-H-A-L-K, chalk is so much fun!

(sung to the tune of "Bingo")

I like to draw things with my chalk.
I draw with chalk on [paper].
C-H-A-L-K! C-H-A-L-K! C-H-A-L-K!
I'll draw with chalk today!

Wet or Dry?

Brush up students' comparison skills with this small-group activity! To begin, give each student the following: two paper plates, a piece of colored chalk, a paintbrush, and a container of water. Have each student make a chalk drawing on one of his plates. Next, have the student use his brush to saturate the center of his second plate with water. Then encourage him to draw a picture on the wet plate. Have each student compare the two drawings by describing the differences in color and texture. Record each student response on the chalkboard. After each group has completed the activity, discuss students' wet and dry observations. Look how chalk changes!

Just add water;
Spray it all about!
Then watch closely
As the chalk spreads out!

Spray It!

Here's another way for your little artists to compare wet and dry chalk drawings! Have each child use chalk to draw an ice-cream cone on both halves of a folded sheet of construction paper. Review students' observations from "Wet or Dry?" Then have the child predict what might happen if she sprays one of her drawings with water. Provide the child with a spray bottle filled with water; then have her saturate one of her drawings as she chants the rhyme below. When everyone has finished, engage your youngsters in a discussion about the similarities and differences of each set of ice-cream cones. As a finishing touch, hang the ice-cream chalk drawings up for a cool display!

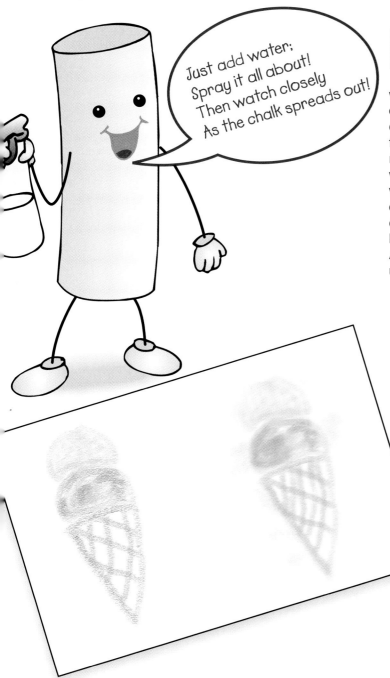

This Is Why

When chalk is applied to a surface, the chalk molecules are crowded together in a close space. If water is added to the surface, the molecules of chalk are able to spread apart. This process is called *diffusion*.

Chalk-Dust Daisies

Fascinate your youngsters with another diffusion activity that will result in beautiful summer flowers! In advance, gather several large pieces of chalk, each a different color. Crush each piece into a powder and then place each color in a separate container. Duplicate the daisy pattern on page 57 for each child. Place the patterns at a center along with a supply of eyedroppers, plastic magnifying glasses, and small cups of water. Invite each child to sprinkle chalk powder onto a daisy pattern and then use an eyedropper to add water to one daisy petal. Next, have him use a magnifying glass to observe the wet powder and the dry powder. Have him compare the two powders; then encourage him to diffuse the powder on the rest of his daisy. Brighten up your classroom by displaying these colorful pastel daisies!

Floating Chalk

Does chalk float? Use this experiment and find out! To begin, have students predict whether or not a piece of chalk will float. Then drop a large piece of chalk into a clear container of water. It sinks! Next, crush the piece of chalk and sprinkle it into the container of water. This time the chalk will float! As an extension, place a piece of paper on the water for approximately 30 seconds. Carefully take the paper out of the water and have students examine the design created by the floating chalk. If desired, place the materials at a center and invite students to create their own chalk designs on paper. Your students will be amazed at their chalk discoveries!

This Is Why

The water has *surface tension*, a force on the water's surface that causes the droplets to stick together. Chalk shavings are light enough to float on the surface of the water without breaking the tension. A whole piece of chalk, however, will sink because it is too heavy for the surface tension to hold.

Nibble on Nutrition!

Serve your youngsters a healthy portion of these nifty nutrition-related activities.

The Incredible Edible Pyramid

Guide your students to good eating habits with this discovery activity. In advance, collect a variety of plastic food, empty food containers, and pictures of food to represent each food group. Place these items in a plastic tub. Then draw a large food pyramid on bulletin board paper with spaces large enough to put the food items or pictures, as shown. If desired, introduce youngsters to the Food Guide Pyramid by reading *The Edible Pyramid: Good Eating Every Day* by Loreen Leedy (Holiday House, Inc.). Next, lay the food pyramid on the floor. Help students sort the items and place each one on the appropriate section of the pyramid. Discuss with your students the food groups and serving sizes. Explain that many favorite foods, such as pizza, are a combination of food groups. Lead them to conclude that the food pyramid is a good guide to help us choose a variety of foods to keep our bodies healthy. For more practice, place the tub of plastic food, pictures, and the pyramid chart in a center for students to sort on their own. That stacks up to nutrition knowledge!

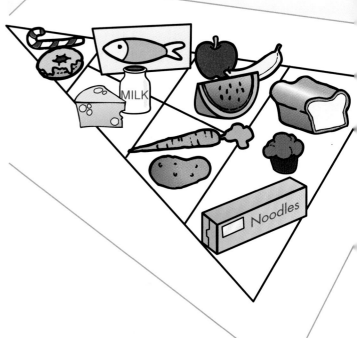

A Pyramid Puzzle

Reinforce food-group recognition and promote healthy eating habits with this tasteful student-made display. In advance, draw a large food pyramid on bulletin board paper and label each food group. Then cut the pyramid into six puzzlelike sections. Gather a class supply of white paper and fingerpaint. Divide your class into six teams and give each team a different food-group puzzle piece. Ask each child to fingerpaint onto white paper a food that belongs to his team's assigned food group. When the paint is dry, ask each team member to cut out his painting and then glue it onto the puzzle piece. Then lay all the puzzle pieces on the floor and have students arrange them into the food pyramid. Explain that the food pyramid is like a puzzle; all the pieces must be present for the pyramid to be complete. In the same way, we need a variety of foods from every food group to maintain a healthy body. Display the finished class project on a bulletin board titled "Pyramid Power."

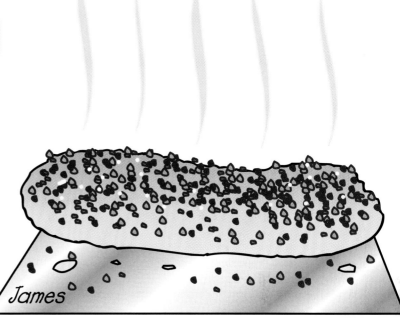

Bodacious Bread

Energize your young nutritionists with this easy bread-baking activity that features the "energy group" of the food pyramid—the bread, cereal, rice, and pasta group. To prepare, defrost enough frozen bread dough so that each child has a small portion. Also gather aluminum foil and small bowls of wheat germ and oatmeal. Discuss foods included in this group; then explain that these foods provide the types of nutrients that give the body the most energy. Direct each child to wash his hands. Then give him a portion of bread dough and a personalized square of aluminum foil. Invite each youngster to twist and roll the dough and then roll it in wheat germ or oatmeal. Place each aluminum foil square on a cookie sheet and bake the bread creations following the package directions. Mmmm, tastes good!

James

Fruit Group

Everybody Loves Fruit

Teach your youngsters the yummy rhyme below and they will be eager to create this fruitful big book! If desired, ask volunteers to provide a variety of washed and cut fresh fruit to share. As your students nibble, explain that fruit helps fight sickness and provides vitamins that promote growth and healthy skin. Following the tasting party, use the text of the rhyme to create the book. Print each line of the poem on the bottom of a separate 12" x 18" piece of construction paper. Ask small groups of children to illustrate each page. If desired, laminate the pages for durability; then sequence the pages and bind them with metal rings or yarn. Share this mouthwatering big book with your youngsters and then place it at the book center. How sweet it is!

I love grapes and tangerines,
Fabulous fruits like nectarines,
Blackberries, strawberries, blueberries, too.
A peach for me and a pear for you!
Piles of fruit heaped on my tray,
I eat two fruit servings every day!

I love grapes and tangerines,

Eating a Rainbow

Introduce your youngsters to colorful snacks that are healthy, too! Foods from the vegetable group come in all shapes, sizes, and colors and contain vitamins that help heal cuts and bruises. In advance, ask parents to donate a variety of fresh vegetables. Make sure you have as many different colors of vegetables as possible. Have the class compare the shapes and sizes of the vegetables and then sort them by color. Then teach your little ones the veggie verse below. Challenge students to name different vegetables to include in the veggie verse. Later, treat your students to a rainbow snack of vegetable tidbits!

Vegetables are so good to eat.
Eating a rainbow just can't be beat!

[Carrots] are so good to eat.
Those [orange] veggies can't be beat!
(Substitute a different vegetable and its color each time you repeat the verse above.)

Vegetables are so good to eat.
Eating a rainbow just can't be beat!

In the "Moo-ood" for Milk

Set the "moo-ood" for learning about dairy products by tempting your tots with a milk taste test. In advance, copy the glass patterns on page 63 to make a class supply; then cut them out. Ask volunteers to donate two different flavors of milk and a class supply of cups. To begin, review the dairy section of the Food Guide Pyramid. Explain that dairy products are important because they contain calcium, which builds strong bones and healthy teeth. Ask youngsters to predict which of the two milk flavors will be the class favorite. Record their answers on chart paper. Next, invite each child to taste each flavor of milk. Have each child write her name on a glass pattern and color it to resemble her favorite flavor. Then ask each child to place her glass in the appropriate row of a graph labeled with the two flavors of milk. Count the results and compare them with students' predictions.

Which flavor of milk will be the favorite?

Chocolate   Strawberry

Ryan   Ashley
Michael   Alex
Michele
Cindy

Milk Favorites Graph

Chocolate   Strawberry

60

Protein Power

Are your little ones full of energy? Where does it all come from? The foods in the meat, poultry, fish, dry beans, eggs, and nuts group are packed with proteins that provide energy. Review the food pyramid as you explain that this group includes foods from animals and plants. Ask students to brainstorm a list of various kinds of protein foods and record their answers on chart paper. Then teach your little ones the following chant and repeat it using protein words from the chart.

Proteins, proteins, good for me.
Proteins give me energy!

[Tuna fish, tuna fish], good for me.
[Tuna fish] gives me energy!

Protein Power

chicken	catfish
turkey	shrimp
meat loaf	chicken soup
hamburgers	boiled eggs
fried eggs	

On the Spot

Help your youngsters spot the fat hidden in some of their favorite snacks with this experiment. To begin, give each child a sheet of white paper and some foods from this group, such as a piece of buttered popcorn, a cookie, and a potato chip. Ask each child to write her name on the paper and then put the foods on it. After a few minutes, have each child remove the food and hold her paper up to the light to see that there are visible oil spots. Tell your students that the spots came from the fat in the food. Review the food pyramid so your youngsters understand that the top section is small to remind us to eat only a few of these foods. Explain that fat is hidden in sweets and snack foods. Even though these foods taste good, they have few nutrients needed for good health. How's that for being on the spot?

James

Home Learning Lab

It is recommended that children eat at least five fruit and/or vegetable servings each day. Give parents the opportunity to focus on their children's balanced diets with this take-home activity. Duplicate the letter on page 64 and the awards on page 63 to make a class supply. Cut out the awards and set them aside. At the end of the week, send home a copy of the letter with each child. When the sheets have been returned, review them with your students, emphasizing their healthy food choices. To reward each child for her healthy eating habits, give each child an award to color and then tape to her clothing.

A Healthy Go-Getter

Now that your little ones are more familiar with nutritious foods, try this activity to encourage healthy food choices. In advance, pack two lunch bags: one with healthy foods, such as carrot sticks, cheese cubes, and a fruit juice box; and the other with less healthy foods, such as potato chips, cookies, and a soft drink. Lay the food pyramid (used in "The Incredible Edible Pyramid" on page 58) on the floor and have your little ones gather around it. Hold up both lunch bags as you sing the song below. Then invite volunteers to put each item on the appropriate section of the food pyramid after you take it out of the bag. Discuss with your students which snack bag contained the healthier choices. Then explain that the carrots, cheese cubes, and fruit juice are nutritious foods that will promote good health. The sugary snacks, even though they taste good, do not help bodies grow and stay healthy. Challenge your youngsters to be healthy go-getters every day!

(sung to the tune of "Did You Ever See a Lassie?")

Here I have two snack bags,
Two snack bags, two snack bags.
Here I have two snack bags,
Let's see what's inside!
Which snack would be better for a healthy go-getter?
Here I have two snack bags,
Let's see what's inside!

Healthy or Not?

Your little ones can share their healthy food findings with these "What Is Healthy? What Is Not?" booklets. In advance, duplicate page 65 for each child. Cut apart the cover and the text strips. Provide each child with a cover, a set of text strips, and five additional half sheets of paper. Have each child glue each of her text strips on a separate half sheet of paper. Then have her sequence the cover and pages before stapling them together along the left side. To complete her book, have her color the cover. Then have the child cut out magazine pictures of three healthy foods and two unhealthy foods. Next, direct her to glue the appropriate pictures to the booklet pages. Invite youngsters to share their books during circle time before taking them home to read to their parents.

What Is Healthy?
What Is Not?

by
Janet

Award Pattern
Use with "Home Learning Lab" on page 61.

Give me five!

I eat 5 servings of fruits or vegetables every day!

©2000 The Education Center, Inc.

Dear Parent,

    We have been studying the Food Guide Pyramid and healthy food choices. Your child has learned that to grow and stay healthy at least five servings of fruits and vegetables should be eaten every day. To promote good eating habits, please help your child complete this handy activity that records how many fruit and vegetable servings he/she eats in a day. First, trace your child's hand on this sheet. On the day of your choice, have your child color in one finger for each fruit or vegetable serving he/she eats. Give your child a "hand" for a job well done!

    Please return this sheet on _____. Thank you for encouraging good eating habits at home and supporting your child's learning!

Trace your child's hand here.

©2000 The Education Center, Inc. • *Science for All Seasons* • Summer • TEC3050

64   **Note to the teacher:** Use with "Home Learning Lab" on page 61.

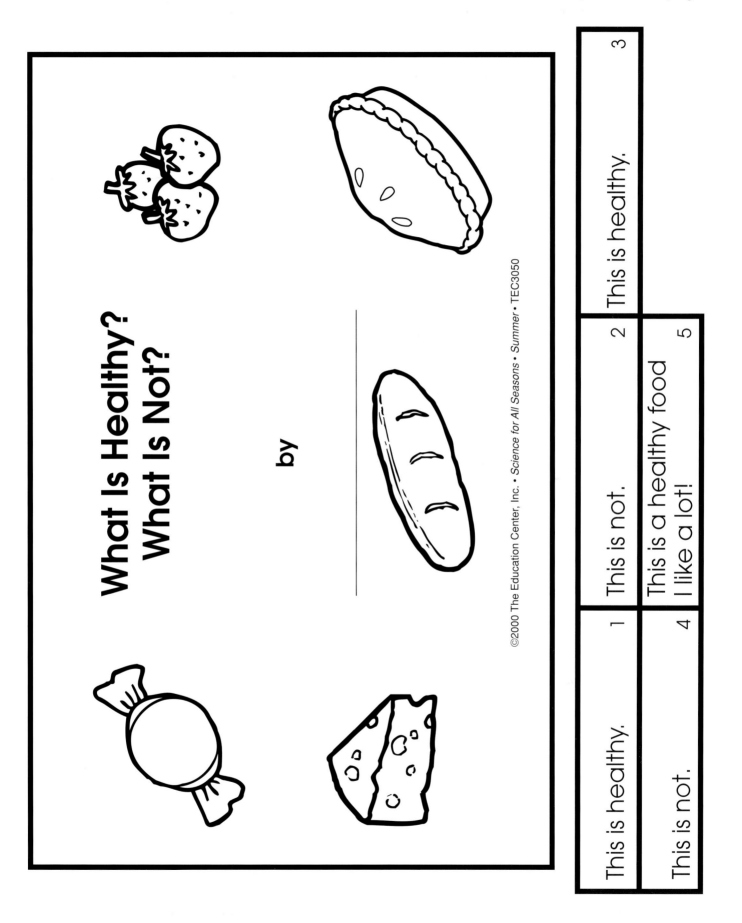

What Is Healthy? What Is Not?

by

_____

©2000 The Education Center, Inc. • *Science for All Seasons* • *Summer* • TEC3050

3	This is healthy.

2	This is not.

5	This is a healthy food I like a lot!

1	This is healthy.

4	This is not.

Sound All Around

Capture the attention of your youngsters with these hands-on activities and make the concept of sound loud and clear to all!

Let's Make Some Noise!

Rev up your youngsters with this sound literature activity! After reading *Too Much Noise* by Ann McGovern (Houghton Mifflin Company), have students recall the noises from the story. Then invite students to take turns creating the noises. Next, have each student name additional noises or noisy items. Record each response on a piece of chart paper. Display the chart in your room and add to it throughout the unit. Happy, noisy sounds will abound!

MEOW!

Too Much

elephants

waterfall

mom yelling

growling bear

The Science of Sound

More noise on the way! Have each student place his hand on his throat and say a few sentences. Next, have each student feel his throat while he is quiet. Discuss the differences and then explain that the movements he feels when he talks are his vocal cords moving back and forth. Explain that the movements are called *vibrations*. Encourage each student to compare the vibrations when he speaks softly to the vibrations when he speaks loudly. Your class will be tingling with good vibrations!

More Vibrations!

Vibrations will resound all over your classroom when you have students try out this simple experiment! In advance, gather several craft sticks, various plastic utensils, and plastic rulers in a variety of lengths. Demonstrate to a small group how to place an item on a table so that an inch or two is beyond the table's surface as shown. Then hold the other end of the ruler on the table. Have each student predict what will happen when the extended part is gently flicked *(the flicked end will move or vibrate)*. Then have students test each item. Next, challenge students to create different sounds with each item by varying the lengths that extend beyond the table. Afterward, have students discuss the different sounds created.

This Is Why

When shorter lengths vibrate slowly, they make a lower sound. Longer lengths make a higher sound. The sounds are called *pitches*.

Catching Waves

Exactly how does sound get to our ears? In invisible waves through the air! Use this small-group activity to help demonstrate how sound travels. To begin, have students in a small group close their eyes. Then strike a bell or triangle one time and have students listen to the sound. Next, invite students to discuss what they heard. Explain that the sound moved from the bell to their ears in invisible waves through the air.

To help demonstrate this concept, place a plastic bowl filled with water on a table. Then, when the water is still, have a student touch the top of the water as you simultaneously strike the bell. As your little ones observe the ripples in the water, explain that just as the waves are moving through the water, invisible sound waves are moving through the air into their ears. How amazing!

KITTY • KITTY • KITTY

67

Danglers

Your youngsters will be up to their ears in fun with this center activity! In advance, prepare several types of danglers (see the box below for directions). Then place them at a center. Direct each student to choose a dangler. Next, have her wrap one end of the string around each index finger and then place each finger in one of her ears. Have her gently swing the item against a table and listen for a sound. Encourage her to try out all of the danglers to see if each item makes a different-pitched sound. Your little ones will want to visit this center over and over to hear the striking sounds!

To make a dangler, tie any of the following objects to the middle of a four-foot length of string:
metal spoon
socket wrench
potato masher
metal ladle
beaters

This Is Why
Sound travels through air and solids. String and wire are the best examples of how vibrations travel through solids.

loud—Boom!
quiet—Shhh
silly—Boing!
scary—Bang!

Making Noise!

Crash! Shhh! Whoosh! Bang! Some noises are loud and some are soft. Use this activity and song to get your youngsters making joyful noises. To begin, have your little ones brainstorm different types of sounds, such as loud, quiet, silly, or scary. Write their responses on a chart and then invite students to brainstorm specific noises to correspond with each type of sound. For example, the noise "Bang!" may correspond with a *scary* sound. Next, sing the song below, replacing the underlined word, in turn, with words from the chart. After each verse, have students make the corresponding sound. What wonderful noise!

(sung to the tune of "Do You Know the Muffin Man?")

Oh, I can make a [quiet] noise,
A [quiet] noise, a [quiet] noise.
Oh, I can make a [quiet] noise.
Listen; here it is!

Hear, Hear!

Give your students' ears a workout with this fun activity! To begin, divide students into pairs; then provide each pair with a length of plastic or rubber tubing (available at your local hardware store). Have one student use the tube to whisper to a partner while his partner listens on the other end. Then have students switch roles. Explain that quiet sounds such as a whisper can be heard through the tube because the air in the tube allows the sound waves to travel.

Underwater?

Pick up the tempo by having your little learners explore sound waves—underwater! In advance, fill a plastic tub with water. Have one child in a small group strike two wooden blocks together in the air. Then have him bang the blocks together under the water while another child puts his ear to the outside of the tub. After each student has experimented, discuss how the sounds were different. Students will agree that sounds are louder underwater. Blub, blub, blub!

This Is Why

Sound not only travels through air, but through water as well. Water carries the sound better, which is why the blocks sound much louder when banged together underwater.

The Rubber Band Brigade

This activity will keep your youngsters' little fingers busy while they learn more about sound! In advance, gather several different-sized rubber bands and a variety of small boxes. Discuss the danger of using rubber bands improperly. Then supervise a small group of students and have each child try out a variety of sound-making techniques, such as plucking the rubber band with her finger and rubbing her chin over it. Have the child use the same technique with different rubber bands so that she can compare the sounds. When everyone has completed the activity, encourage each student to stretch some rubber bands over the opening of a box and play it like an instrument. Listen to that music!

This Is Why

When the rubber bands are plucked, they vibrate and make sounds. The sound of a rubber band depends on its size. Lower sounds are made by thicker rubber bands and higher sounds are produced by thin rubber bands.

What Do You Hear?

Bees buzzing, thunder rumbling, cars zooming, geese honking. Sounds are all around us! Your youngsters will be in tune with sounds after this class book project. In advance, duplicate page 72 to make a class supply of the booklet page. Read *Polar Bear, Polar Bear, What Do You Hear?* by Bill Martin Jr. (Henry Holt and Company) and then discuss the sounds heard in the story. Have students brainstorm other things that make sounds. Record student responses on a piece of chart paper. Then have each student choose a different word from the list and draw that item on her booklet page. Assist her in completing the sentences on her booklet page. Then have her glue a small picture (or a photocopy of a school picture) in the labeled square. Stack the completed pages between two covers and staple them together along the left side. What do you hear in your reading area? Laughter and enjoyment!

Sherri
(name)

What do you hear?

I hear a
radio
(noun)

blasting
(action verb)

in my ear!

SOU

duck	birds
car	staple
train	compu
thunder	phone
whistle	cat
rain	baby
flute	feet

Home Learning Lab

Strengthen the home-school connection by having families work together to make this unusual sound maker! In advance, duplicate page 71 to make a class supply. Send a note home with each student, inviting parents to make a tapping tube with their child. Encourage each child to bring his tube to school. Then gather together your little ones and their tubes. (Be sure to have extra tubes for those children unable to make one.) Invite each child to tap his tube on a towel or piece of carpet and then compare the sounds of the different-sized tubes. Tap, tap away!

Fun With Drums!

Drum up some excitement in your classroom with this hands-on rhythm activity! In advance, cut a supply of 12" x 12" brown paper grocery bag squares. Gather a variety of rubber bands; plastic grocery bags; and clean, empty containers, such as oatmeal boxes, coffee cans, and sturdy margarine tubs. Have each student choose a container and then assist him in covering it with a paper bag square or a plastic bag. Then secure the covering with a rubber band, making sure it is smooth, with no wrinkles. Invite each child to play his drum for the class; then have students discuss the different sounds. As an extension, invite groups of students to use their drums to make different sounds and rhythms together. Use the tapping tube instruments from "Home Learning Lab" and you will have quite a little band!

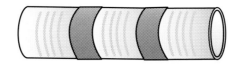

Tap, Tap, Tapping Tube

Parents! Team up with your child and create this unusual sound maker! After completing the project, have your child bring it to school.

You will need:

several clean, same-sized cans (tomato paste, soup, large juice cans, etc.); duct tape or packaging tape; a can opener; and a towel

Instructions:

1. Cut the bottoms off all the cans but one. Cover any sharp edges with tape.

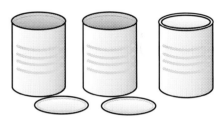

2. Tape the cans together to make a tube. The can with the bottom will be the base of the tube. If desired, decorate the tube with stickers or other art supplies.

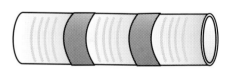

3. Put a towel on the floor. Hold your tapping tube with the open end up and tap it on the towel. Try tapping your tube on other surfaces, such as a side-walk and a doormat.

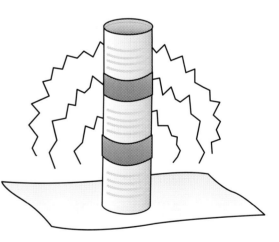

What Happens?

When the tube is tapped on a surface, the cans vibrate, causing sound. The number of cans used to make the tube determines the sound it makes. Longer tubes make lower sounds, while shorter tubes make higher sounds.

_____ ,
(name)

_____ ,

What do you hear?

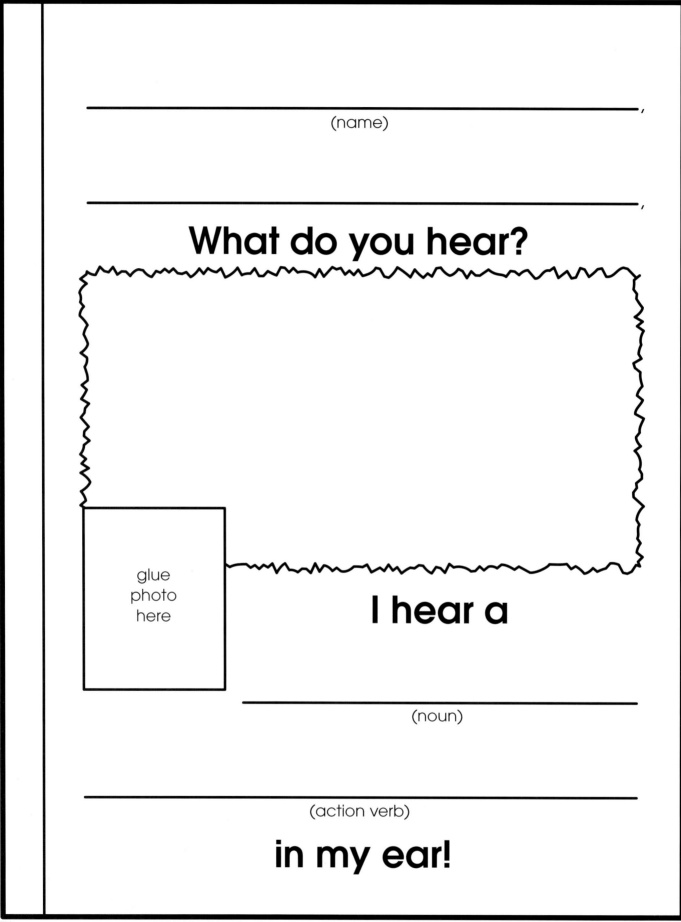

glue
photo
here

I hear a

_____
(noun)

_____
(action verb)

in my ear!

Wild About Water

Dive right into these science-oriented activities about water. Your students will be in the swim of things in no time!

Shape Up!

Splash into your water studies with this center activity that introduces youngsters to a basic property of water. In advance, make a copy of the reporting sheet (page 78) for each child. Next, gather four different-shaped plastic containers or sand molds. Place the containers at your water table or near a large bucket filled with water. If desired, tint the water with red food coloring. Next, place the reporting sheets and a supply of pencils and crayons near the water table. Invite a small group of youngsters to visit the center and pour the water from one container into another. Encourage each child to observe the shape of the water in each container. Then have the child record her observations on a recording sheet. After each child has had an opportunity to visit this center, discuss students' findings.

This Is Why
Water is a liquid. It does not have its own shape, and flows freely, taking the shape of its new container.

This Is Why
Objects appear larger through the water droplets because they are curved outward, just like the lens in a magnifying glass.

Now See This!

Can a water droplet be used as a magnifying glass? Try this easy experiment and see! Give each child in a small group a half sheet of newspaper and a square of waxed paper. Have the child place her waxed paper on the newspaper. Then have her use an eyedropper to drop water on the waxed paper. Next, instruct the child to slowly move the waxed paper across the newspaper and watch the print through the water. Your young scientists will be amazed to discover that the print is enlarged!

Sink or Float?

Does it sink or does it float? Like a rock or like a boat? Youngsters will discover the answers to these questions with this center and booklet idea. In advance, gather everyday objects for youngsters to test (see the list to the right for suggestions). Then set them at your water table. Next, photocopy the data sheets on page 80 to make a supply. Place the sheets near your water table along with a supply of crayons and pencils. Invite each student to test each object to see if it will sink or float. Then have the child record the results by drawing the object on a data sheet and coloring the appropriate face. When the child has tested all of the objects, have her stack her data sheets. Place a copy of the booklet cover (page 79) on top and then staple the pages along the left side. Invite the child to color and personalize the cover and then take her booklet home to share with her family.

feathers
corks
pencils
soap bars
keys
marbles
markers
combs
sponges
rocks
toy boats
paper clips
empty plastic
    bottles
string
toothbrushes
scissors
craft sticks

Float Your Boat

Need a creative activity that will help students practice problem-solving skills? Stock a center near your water table with foil, balsa wood, Styrofoam® trays, and play dough. Challenge each of your little ones to build a boat that will hold five counting cubes without sinking. Encourage youngsters to construct and test boats of different sizes and shapes. After each child has successfully constructed his boat, issue another challenge: how many cubes will it take to sink his boat?

"Can-damonium"

Further your float studies with this surprising demonstration. In advance, gather one can of diet soda and one can of regular soda. Then fill a large clear container with water. Have students predict whether or not the cans will float. Record student predictions on a chart; then place the cans in the water. Your little ones may be surprised to discover that one can floats and one can sinks! Now how did that happen?

This Is Why

The carbonated water in the diet soda makes it float. Regular soda also contains carbonated water, too, but it also contains a large amount of sugar. The sugar makes the soda too dense to float. Diet sodas do not contain sugar, and, therefore, they will float.

74

Bottled Up

Your little ones will be eager to try their hands at this outdoor water activity! In advance, collect several empty plastic bottles, each with a lid. Set the bottles near large buckets filled with water. Invite each child to push a bottle under the water. Then have the student observe what happens when the bottle is released. It will float! Next, direct the child to fill the bottles with water and repeat the experiment. This time the bottle will sink! After your students have completed this activity, lead them to conclude that the air in the first bottle kept it afloat. (For an extension activity, see "Sink the Bottle" on page 76.)

The Air Necessities

Continue to explore how air helps things float with this fruitful idea. In advance, gather a lemon, a grapefruit, a banana, and an apple. Show each fruit to your group and have students predict whether or not each will float. Record student predictions on a chart similar to the one shown. Next, have a student volunteer place each fruit in the water. Your little ones will discover that they float! Next, remove the fruit from the water and peel each one. Ask youngsters again to predict whether or not each fruit will float or sink. Record student predictions; then place the peeled fruit in the water. This time they sink! Review the conclusion from "Bottled Up" above. *(Air in the bottle kept it afloat.)* Then have youngsters brainstorm reasons why the unpeeled fruit floated and the peeled fruit sank.

This Is Why

The peels of the fruits have tiny bubbles of air in them. The air causes the fruit to float. When the fruits are peeled, they sink.

	predictions (unpeeled)	results (unpeeled)	predictions (peeled)	results (peeled)
🍋				
🍊				
🍌				
🍎				

Sink the Bottle

Little ones will love this outdoor activity that focuses on observation, prediction, and measurement skills. In advance, place the following near a large bucket of water: a container of sand, a one-cup measuring cup, a funnel, and an empty bottle with a lid. Invite students to predict the number of cups of sand needed to sink the bottle. Then have them count the actual number needed. If desired, repeat the activity using different-sized bottles.

Sticky Drops

Here's a center activity that will certainly keep the attention of your youngsters! To prepare, tape a length of plastic wrap to a table. Stock the center with eyedroppers, flat wooden toothpicks, a supply of paper towels (for easy cleanup), and a shallow bowl of tinted water. Invite each child to fill her eyedropper with water and then squeeze a drop onto the plastic. The water drop will roll around on the plastic. Next, invite her to squeeze several more drops of water onto the plastic; then push the drops together with the side of a toothpick. What happens when water droplets get very near each other? They combine and form a bigger drop of water! How big a water drop can each of your little scientists make?

This Is Why
Water is cohesive. When one water drop meets another, they combine, forming a bigger drop of water.

Weight Watchers

This center activity has youngsters soaking up some measurement practice! To prepare, cover a table with a plastic tablecloth. Then place at the table a balance scale, counting blocks, a bucket of water, and a variety of absorbent objects such as sponges and paper towels. Invite each child to use the counting blocks and scale to weigh one of the objects. Next, direct him to dunk the object in the water, remove it, and then weigh it again. The object will weigh more! Invite the child to repeat the activity with the remaining objects; then lead him to conclude that each object weighed more the second time because it had absorbed some water.

Over the Top

Trying this small-group activity will be heaps of fun for little hands. To begin, provide each child in a small group with a five-ounce plastic cup, a plastic plate or tray, and a supply of marbles. Have the child place his cup on the plate; then use a pitcher of water to fill his cup to the top. Direct the child to carefully add marbles, one at a time, to his cup. As each marble is added, encourage the child to observe the water from the side of the cup. After a few marbles have been added, guide him to notice the water level rising over the rim of the cup, but not spill over! As an extension, invite students to continue adding marbles until the water spills over the edge of their cups. Have each child count the number of marbles needed to spill the water and then compare the results.

This Is Why

There is a special force on the water's surface, *surface tension*, that causes the water droplets to stick together. The surface tension is so strong that the water can rise above the top of the cup without spilling. The water finally spills when it gets so high that the force can no longer keep the droplets together.

Traveling Water

Discover how water can travel on its own when your water enthusiasts dive into this science investigation! To begin, provide each child in a small group with a foil pie pan, one facial tissue, and a personalized three-ounce paper cup. Half-fill each child's cup with water; then carefully set his cup on the edge of a table. Next, direct the child to twist his tissue. Have him place one end of the tissue in the water and hang the other end off the edge of the table. Next, place a pie pan on the floor directly below the tissue. Ask youngsters to predict what will happen to the water and the tissue. Then have them carefully observe the water and tissue. In just a few minutes, youngsters will be thrilled to discover that the water has moved up the tissue! After approximately 30 minutes, the water will begin to drip from the tissue into the pie pan. Encourage students to discuss the results and possible explanations.

Home Learning Lab

Strengthen your home-school bond with this simple take-home activity. Send home a copy of the parent note (page 81) with each child. Then, at bath time, youngsters and parents will splish-splash in a scientific way!

Name _____

Draw the shape the water takes in each container.

1	2
3	4

Sink or Float?

Does it sink?
Or does it float?
Like a rock?
Or like a boat?

by

_____

Sink or Float?

Does it sink?
Or does it float?
Like a rock?
Or like a boat?

by

_____

Data Sheet

Use with "Sink or Float?" on page 74.

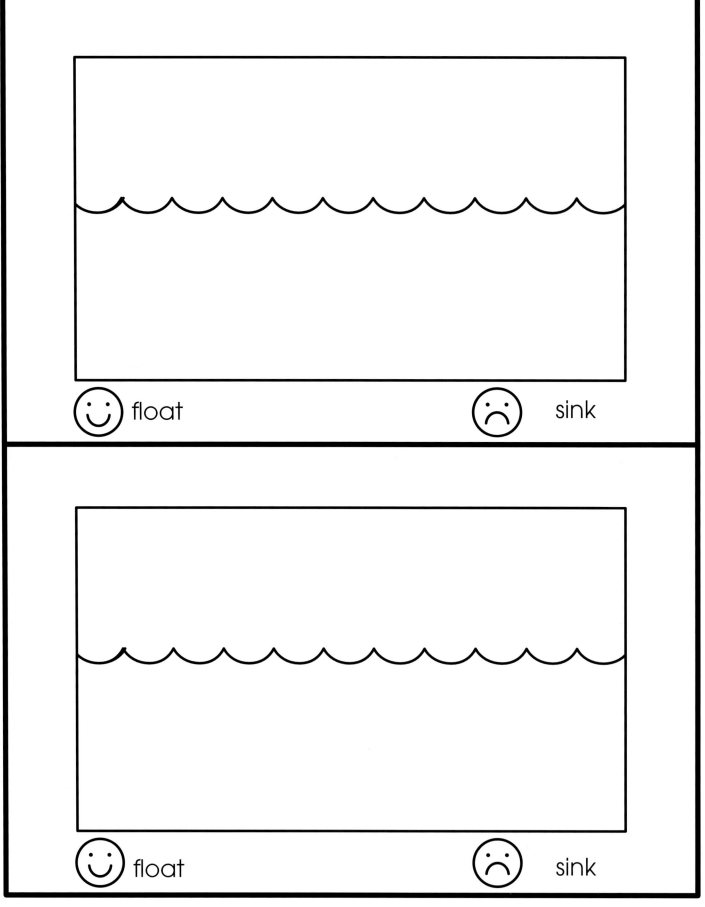

float   sink

float   sink

Splish-Splash Science in the Tub

Dear Parents,
    The next time it's bath time, try these simple water experiments with your child:

Rising Water
Before your child hops in the bathtub, mark the level of the water with a piece of duct tape. Then invite your little one to climb in. Watch to see how far the water rises!

Historical Tidbit
More than 2,000 years ago, a Greek mathematician and inventor named Archimedes noticed that when he got into his bathtub, the water level rose. His observation led to the Archimedes Principle, which states that an object immersed in fluid loses weight equal to the weight of the amount of fluid it displaces.

Bubbling Sponge
Give your child a new sponge to play with in the tub. Does it float? Squeeze the sponge under the water. What comes out of the sponge?

What Happened?
Sponges contain many airholes; that's why they float. When a sponge is squeezed under water, air bubbles are forced out into the water.

Flower Power

Did you know that flowers have the power to help little ones' observation skills grow? After completing this bunch of activities, your students are sure to pick this flower study as a favorite!

Just Look at Those Flowers!

You'll want some fresh flowers for little ones to study, so purchase a class supply—plus four or five extra—of inexpensive white daisies. (You might even get a local florist to donate some.) Collect a class supply of small plastic soda bottles with lids. Use an ice pick to punch a hole in each lid; then partially fill the bottles with water and screw the lids on tightly. Use a permanent marker to write a different child's name on each bottle. Then insert a daisy into the hole in the lid of each bottle. Place the extra daisies in a vase of water for use with other activities in this unit.

Give each child a daisy in a bottle. Invite youngsters to look closely at their daisies and report on the colors, shapes, and textures they discover. Write their descriptions on a flower-shaped piece of chart paper. Set the chart aside to be used on the display described in "Draw a Daisy." And keep the daisies handy for the other activities on this page and page 83.

The middle is yellow.—Katie

It's got leaves.—Gabi

Mine is pretty!—Louis

There are white petals. They are oval.—Justin

Meghan

Daisy Details

Encourage your young scientists to delve into details by asking them to study a daisy piece by piece. In advance, photocopy the patterns on pages 86 and 87. Color the flower center, leaves, and stem; then prepare all the pieces for use on your flannelboard. Gather your group around the flannelboard and show them a real daisy that has a stem and at least one leaf. Name the parts of the daisy—*stem, leaf, petals,* and *center*—as you point to them on your flower. Next, line up the prepared pieces along the bottom of your flannelboard. Ask student volunteers to help assemble this flannelboard flower puzzle to make a complete daisy. Wrap things up by placing each vocabulary card on the board next to its matching part. Then have students find each part on their real flowers. Leave the flannelboard pieces and vocabulary cards in a basket near your flannelboard for students to use independently during center time.

center

petal

stem

leaf

Draw a Daisy

Invite each of your youngsters to draw a portrait of her flower friend! Provide students with bright blue paper and chalk in various colors, including white. Before they begin to draw, review the parts of a daisy with youngsters and talk about the shapes and colors that make up the daisy. Encourage them to fill their entire papers with their daisy drawings. Next, on a bulletin board with a sunny yellow background, mount the flower-shaped chart you made in "Just Look at Those Flowers!" Add your youngsters' finished artwork to the display; then title it "Our Daisy Discoveries."

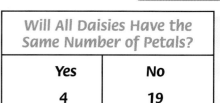

Petal Count

Just how many petals does it take to make a daisy? Challenge each child to examine the petals on her flower to find out! Prior to this activity, duplicate the petal patterns on page 87 to make a class supply. Cut out the petals and keep them handy in a zippered plastic bag. Ask students if they think all their daisies will have the same number of petals or if the number will vary from flower to flower. On your chalkboard, record the votes for each answer. Then have each child look carefully at her flower and estimate, without actually counting, the number of petals on her flower. Then help each student count her flower's petals and record the number on a petal cutout. Was her estimate close to the actual number? When everyone's petals are counted, label a chalkboard graph with the various totals. Have each youngster use a bit of Sticky-Tac to attach her petal cutout to the graph in the appropriate row. Then analyze the results of your counting experiment. What was the greatest number of petals? The smallest number? Ahhh…math skills are in full bloom!

Will All Daisies Have the Same Number of Petals?	
Yes	No
4	19

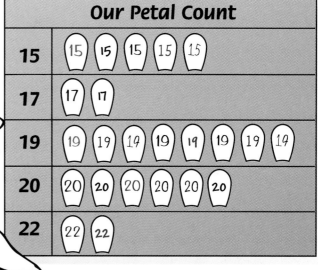

Our Petal Count

15	15 15 15 15 15
17	17 17
19	19 19 19 19 19 19 19 19
20	20 20 20 20 20 20
22	22 22

A Stem Is Like a Straw

Help your little ones see why the stem is an essential part of a flower with this experiment. First, ask each student to remove his daisy from its bottle and carefully inspect the stem. Use a knife to slit the stems (lengthwise) of two extra daisies and lay them out on paper towels. Invite a few students at a time to use magnifying glasses to study the inside structure of these stems. When everyone has had a chance to observe the stems, explain that a flower stem is like a drinking straw. It helps move water from the ground (or vase) up to the leaves and flowers. Carry out this experiment to demonstrate.

Take one of your extra daisies and trim the bottom of the stem; then place the daisy in a cup of blue-tinted water. Take a second extra daisy and tightly wrap the entire stem with aluminum foil, being careful to completely seal the cut end. Place this stem in a cup of blue-tinted water as well. After 6 to 12 hours, your little ones will discover that the once-white petals of the first daisy now are tinted blue! The second daisy will still be white. Ask little ones what happened; then remind them that the stem is like a straw. The stem of the first daisy carried the blue water to the bloom, tinting it blue. The stem of the second daisy couldn't transport any blue water because of the foil seal.

This Is Why

If a stem is like a straw, where does the suction come from? A flower's leaves and petals contain many tiny pores. Water in the flower evaporates into the air through these pores. As the water evaporates, more water is pulled up through the stem of the flower. This process is called *transpiration*.

red

orange

A Rainbow of Color

Of course, flowers come in many beautiful colors besides bright daisy white. Introduce little ones to the range of flower colors by reading *Planting a Rainbow* by Lois Ehlert (Harcourt Brace & Company). After reading the book, ask each child to pick her favorite flower from the story and paint a picture of it on a large sheet of newsprint. When the paintings are dry, have children cut them out. Place all the flower cutouts on the floor and invite youngsters to gather round and help you sort the flowers by color. Complete this classification exercise by displaying the flower paintings in color-sorted bunches on a bulletin board. Add the corresponding color word on a sentence strip near each colorful bouquet.

Put 'em in Pots

For more color classification practice, set up this center for your would-be flower gardeners. To prepare, purchase or ask parents to donate a supply of artificial flowers in a range of colors and several plastic flowerpots (one for each color of flower). Fill the pots with play sand and set them in your sand table. Cut the stems of the artificial flowers so that they fit nicely in the flowerpots; then put them in a large, unbreakable vase near your sand table. Invite youngsters to visit this center to "plant" the flowers, sorting them by color into different flowerpots. Then encourage little ones to "pick" all the flowers and arrange them in the vase as they desire. How lovely!

Sing a Song of Colors

Everyone has a favorite flower color. Invite students to sing this song to tell you about theirs! Sing the song once, inserting *your* name and favorite flower color. Then repeat it, asking a different student to tell you her favorite flower color. Continue to personalize the verse for each child.

(sung to the tune of "The Farmer in the Dell")

Oh, flowers are so bright
And colorful to see!
[Renee] likes flowers all in [yellow],
Pretty as can be!

So Many Seeds!

From asters to zinnias, a wide variety of flowers grows from a wide variety of flower seeds. Use this center idea to sprout a super study of seeds. In advance, purchase packets of different-sized flower seeds (see the list below). At your science center, provide magnifying glasses and one white paper plate with a sprinkling of all the different seeds. Invite youngsters to study the seeds; then add this seed-matching game to the center to develop students' visual-discrimination skills. To prepare, place a sticky dot on the outside of each seed packet. Glue a few of the seeds from inside the packet to the sticky dot. Then glue a few more of the same seeds to an index card. Label the opposite side of the card with the flower name. (Tape the seed packets shut or remove the remaining seeds for other uses.) Place the packets and cards in a basket.

To use the game, a child matches each seed packet to its corresponding index card by looking at the seeds. Kindergartners can check their work by matching the flower names on the packets and the back sides of the cards.

sunflower	morning glory	marigold
nasturtium	zinnia	alyssum

The Planting Process

With all this talk of flowers and seeds, your little ones will definitely want to plant some flowers of their own! So prepare a simple flowerpot for each child by poking three holes in the bottom of a Styrofoam® cup. Label the cup with the child's name. Then soak a class supply of nasturtium seeds overnight. On planting day, invite each child to fill her cup with potting soil to about one inch below the rim. Follow the directions on the seed packet for planting the soaked nasturtium seeds. Then encourage each student to spray her potted seed with water until the soil is quite damp. Seal each child's cup inside a zippered plastic bag and place it in a warm area of your classroom. Encourage youngsters to check on the progress of their plants each day until they begin to sprout. Then remove the cups from the bags, place them in a sunny window, and water the plants as needed. When each plant has grown a few sturdy leaves, invite students to take them home for further observation.

Big News! A Brand-New Nasturtium!

Dear Family:

We have been learning about flowers at school. We've even grown our very own flowers and we're bringing them home today! Please help your child continue to study the growth of his or her nasturtium plant at home. To take care of it, place it in a sunny window and water it when the surface of the soil is dry to the touch. And try these activities to help your budding scientist keep learning!

• Talk about the size, shape, color, and texture of the leaves.
• Measure and compare the biggest and smallest leaves.
• Search for flower buds on the plant.
• Observe and talk about how the flower buds change each day.

When your child's plant has one or more fully opened flowers, have your child draw a picture of it in the space below. Or take a photo of your child holding the plant and glue it to the space below. Have your child bring this letter back to school to show the class the progress of his or her plant.

Home Learning Lab

Once your young scientists have successfully sprouted some nasturtium seeds (see "The Planting Process"), send the plants home for a more long-term study. Photocopy page 88 for each child to take home along with her plant. Parent-and-child learning will blossom as they observe, discuss, and measure their growing plants.

Flannelboard Patterns
Use with "Daisy Details" on page 82.

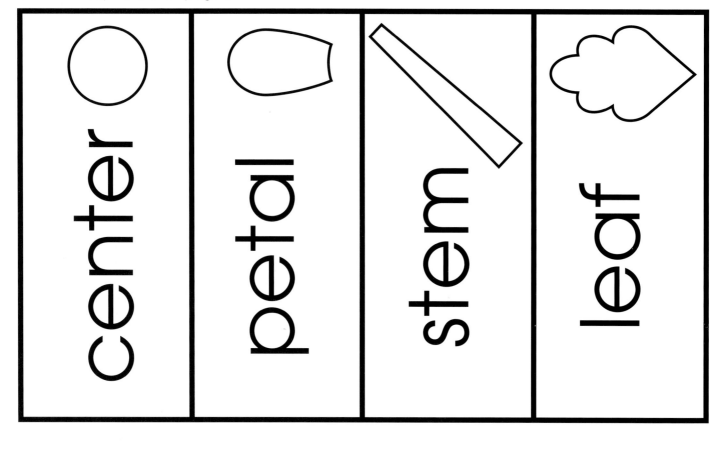

center

petal

stem

leaf

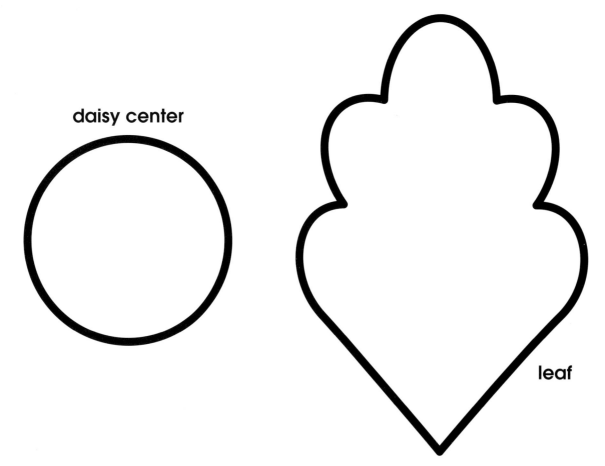

daisy center

leaf

Flannelboard Patterns

Use with "Daisy Details" on page 82. Use petal patterns with "Petal Count" on page 83.

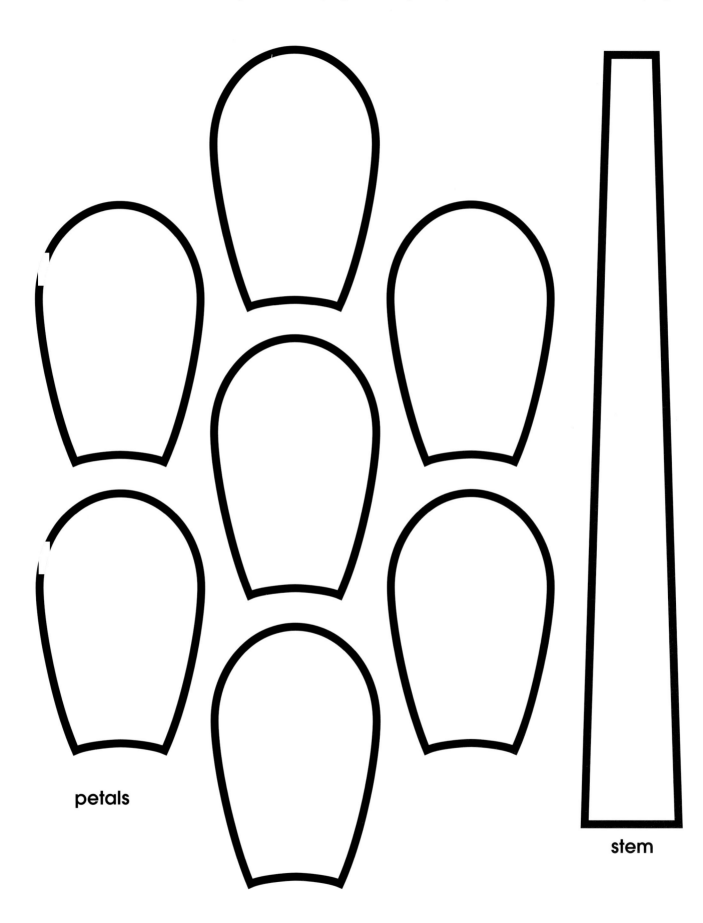

petals

stem

Big News!
A Brand-New Nasturtium!

Dear Family:

We have been learning about flowers at school. We've even grown our very own flowers and we're bringing them home today! Please help your child continue to study the growth of his or her nasturtium plant at home. To take care of it, place it in a sunny window and water it when the surface of the soil is dry to the touch. And try these activities to help your budding scientist keep learning!

• Talk about the size, shape, color, and texture of the leaves.
• Measure and compare the biggest and smallest leaves.
• Search for flower buds on the plant.
• Observe and talk about how the flower buds change each day.

When your child's plant has one or more fully opened flowers, have your child draw a picture of it in the space below. Or take a photo of your child holding the plant and glue it to the space below. Have your child bring this letter back to school to show the class the progress of his or her plant.

Note to the teacher: Use with "Home Learning Lab" on page 85.

Gloppy, Sloppy Goop!

Summertime is tactile time—time for mashing, smashing, ooey-gooey, sticky-icky sensory fun!

Ask the Experts

What's ooey-gooey, squishy, and icky? Ask the experts—your little ones! Begin your study of all things gloppy by asking your group to brainstorm a list of things that they consider gooey. Jot student responses on a chart and then get your group in a gooey frame of mind by singing the song below.

(sung to the tune of "Yankee Doodle")

Hands are mashing,
Fingers squishing,
Toes are wiggling, too,
In a mushy, gushy, sticky mess
That's gooey through and through!

I love gloppy, sloppy stuff!
Let's play with it awhile.
Ooey-gooey, squishy, ick!
It really makes me smile!

Stretch It!

This stretchy, rubbery concoction will have your little ones bouncing with excitement! In advance, gather the materials and supplies listed on the recipe card below; then assist each student in pouring the correct amount of glue into a large plastic cup. Next, have her add several drops of food coloring to the glue. Then slowly pour the liquid starch into each child's cup as she stirs the mixture with a craft stick. Direct the child to continue stirring until a smooth, rubbery putty forms. If the mixture is too sticky, add small amounts of starch until the mixture is smooth. Then have her remove the putty from the cup. If necessary, help the child gently blot the putty with a paper towel to remove excess liquid. Encourage students to make a variety of shapes with the putty and experiment to see if it bounces, stretches, or breaks apart easily. Your youngsters will be amazed at their scientific creations!

Stretchy Putty

Materials and supplies needed for each child:
1/4 c. white glue
1/4 c. liquid starch
several drops of food coloring
large plastic cup
1 craft stick

This Is Why

The putty is a *colloid* that remains in a state of *suspension*. In other words, the starch and the glue particles don't dissolve to form a complete mixture. Other examples of colloids are Jell-O® gelatin, whipped cream, and styling gels.

Oh, Wonderful Mud!

Use this activity to introduce your students to another kind of gloppy, sloppy goop—mud! Begin by reading *Mrs. Wishy-Washy* by Joy Cowley (Philomel Books). After sharing the story, invite students to answer the question "How do you make mud?" Record their responses on a mud puddle–shaped chart; then use the activity below to make a real batch of ooey-gooey mud!

How Do You Make Mud?

"Swish dirty water around real fast."
Joshua

"Leave a bucket of dirt in the rain."
Deanne

"Pour water over your shoes."
Jack

"Pour dirt in a puddle."
Kayla

What Is Mud?

Mud is simply dirt mixed with water. It can be thick or very runny. What's the best recipe for mud? Set up this mud-mixing experiment; then invite small groups of youngsters to work with you and find out. To prepare, gather a bucket of dirt and a pitcher of water. Then provide each child in the group with one small plastic cup, a plastic spoon, and a foil pie pan. Invite each child to fill his cup with dirt and then pour the dirt into his pan. Half-fill the child's cup with water. Then have him stir spoonfuls of water into the dirt until the mud reaches a consistency he desires. Invite the child to explore the mud with his fingers (or spoon) and describe the experience. Thick or thin, making mud will make your students grin!

Mud-Pie Central

Set up a sensory bonanza by filling your empty sand or water table with a pile of wonderful mud. If desired, mix some twigs, leaves, acorns, and small plastic flowers into the mud. Next, place foil tart pans, spoons, and craft sticks at the table; then encourage students to use the supplies to make mud pies. Provide a bucket of water and paper towels so your little pie makers can easily wash up.

Squish, Squish, Squish!

Tout this tune about making mud. Your little mud fans will be singing it in no time!

(sung to the tune of "Six Little Ducks")

Playing in the dirt is fun to do.
Playing in the water is great fun, too!
When you mix dirt and water,
Mud's the dish!
Fingers wiggle-wiggle and go squish, squish, squish!
Squish, squish, squish!
Squish, squish, squish!
Fingers wiggle-wiggle and go squish, squish, squish!

Comparing Mud-Pie Mixtures

Soil, sand, or dirt. Which of these earthy ingredients makes the best mud pie? Use this small-group activity and find out! In advance, place one cup each of sand, packaged potting soil, and regular outdoor dirt in separate bowls. Place the bowls at a table along with a container of water, three spoons, and three Styrofoam® trays. Invite each child in a small group to explore the sand, soil, and dirt. Then have students predict which one might make the best pie! Ask the group members to recall the amount of water they added to a cup of dirt in "What Is Mud?" (page 90) to create just the right muddy mixture. Then have them help you add water to each bowl until it is just the right pie consistency. Next, invite your little ones to use their hands to press each mixture into a separate foam tray. Place the trays in the sun to dry. When the pies are dry, turn them out of their trays onto a sheet of newspaper; then have youngsters observe and discuss the results!

sand   soil   dirt

Just Glue It!

It's gloppy and it's sloppy! It's icky and it's sticky! It's glue! Follow the directions below to create a sample of the sticky stuff; then get gluing!

Materials and supplies needed for each child:
1/4 c. warm milk (not boiling)
1 tbsp. vinegar
1/8 tsp. baking soda
three 7-oz. paper cups
1 coffee filter
1 craft stick

1. Mix the milk and vinegar in a cup; then let the mixture sit until white lumps begin to form (about three minutes).
2. Place a coffee filter in another cup. Pour the mixture through the coffee filter. Then carefully squeeze the filter to remove any excess liquid.
3. Use a craft stick to scrape the solids out of the coffee filter and into a third cup.
4. Add the baking soda to the solids; then stir. Now it's glue!

Will the homemade glue stick? Let the testing begin! Provide each child with two construction paper squares and two squares of aluminum foil. Direct the child to use her craft stick to scrape some glue out of her cup and then glue the paper squares together. Next, have her glue the foil squares together in the same manner. Allow the glue to dry overnight. The next morning, challenge each child to pull the papers and foil apart. Your little ones may be surprised to discover that the glue worked on the paper but not on the foil!

This Is Why

When the vinegar is added to the milk, thick white solids form that contain a protein called *casein* (KAY-seen). The casein sticks to the fibers in the construction paper. Because aluminum foil does not contain fibers, the glue does not stick.

Mash 'n' Smash Snack

Tempt little taste buds with this gloppy, sloppy snack. It's simply smashing!

Ingredients for one snack:
1/2 banana, peeled
4 tsp. thawed frozen strawberries
1/4 c. vanilla yogurt
2 tsp. honey
2 tsp. chopped nuts

Wash your hands. Place the banana and strawberries in a bowl; then use your hands to thoroughly mash the fruit. Wash your hands again. Use a spoon to stir in the yogurt, honey, and nuts; then eat!

From Slurry to Paper

Here's an activity that will have little hands "slop-happy"! To begin, explain to youngsters that a *slurry* is a watery, mushy mixture. Then help small groups of children follow the directions below to create a sloppy slurry that magically transforms into paper!

Materials needed to make one sheet:
1 large bowl
one 10½" x 13½" piece of plastic needlepoint
   canvas cut in half
1 rolling pin
4 c. water
one 8½" x 11" sheet of newsprint
2 facial tissues
1 paper towel
1 small section of a brown paper lunch bag
one-cup measuring cup

1. Invite the group to examine the newsprint, tissues, paper towel, and lunch bag. Have them compare the textures and then tear the paper into tiny pieces.
2. Place two cups of the torn paper into the bowl. (Set aside the remaining paper pieces to use in the booklet activity at right.)
3. Add the water to the bowl; then invite youngsters to mix, mash, and tear the wet paper with their hands.
4. Let the paper soak for several hours until it forms a watery mixture, or *slurry*.
5. Take the bowl of slurry, the rolling pin, and the plastic canvas outside to a sunny, paved area.
6. Lay one piece of canvas on the pavement and pour the slurry onto it.
7. Have a child spread the slurry evenly in the center of the canvas and then place the other piece of canvas on top of the slurry.
8. Invite each child to roll the rolling pin over the canvas to squeeze the water out of the slurry.
9. Place the canvas in the sun to dry for several hours.
10. Peel the dry slurry off the canvas. Presto, you've made paper! Invite youngsters to compare the finished product with the original pieces of torn paper. Then cut the homemade paper into squares and provide each child in the group with a square to use in the booklet activity to the right.

Papermaking Booklet

Now that your little ones have made paper, they'll be ready to record the recipe in their own booklets. To make one booklet, duplicate pages 94–96. Cut apart the booklet pages, sequence them, and then staple them on the left side between construction paper covers. Program the front cover as shown; then have each child follow the directions below to complete the pages.

Cover: Write your name on the line.
Page 1: Glue bits of paper (from "From Slurry to Paper") to the page.
Page 2: Use blue watercolor to paint water pouring out of the pitcher.
Page 3: Color the slurry gray.
Page 4: Color the slurry gray. Use craft glue to glue a small piece of plastic canvas on top of the slurry.
Page 5: Color the sun yellow. Glue on yellow yarn sunbeams.
Page 6: Glue to the page a small square of the paper you made.

This Is Why

Paper is made from bits of fibers that have been pressed together. Tearing and wetting the paper breaks it down into separate fibers again. When the water evaporates, the fibers bond into a solid form of paper once more.

In go bits of paper.
Rip, rip, rip!

1

Now add a little water.
Drip, drip, drip!

2

Make a sloppy slurry.
Mush, mush, mush!

3

Then spread it on a canvas.
Squish, squish, squish!

4

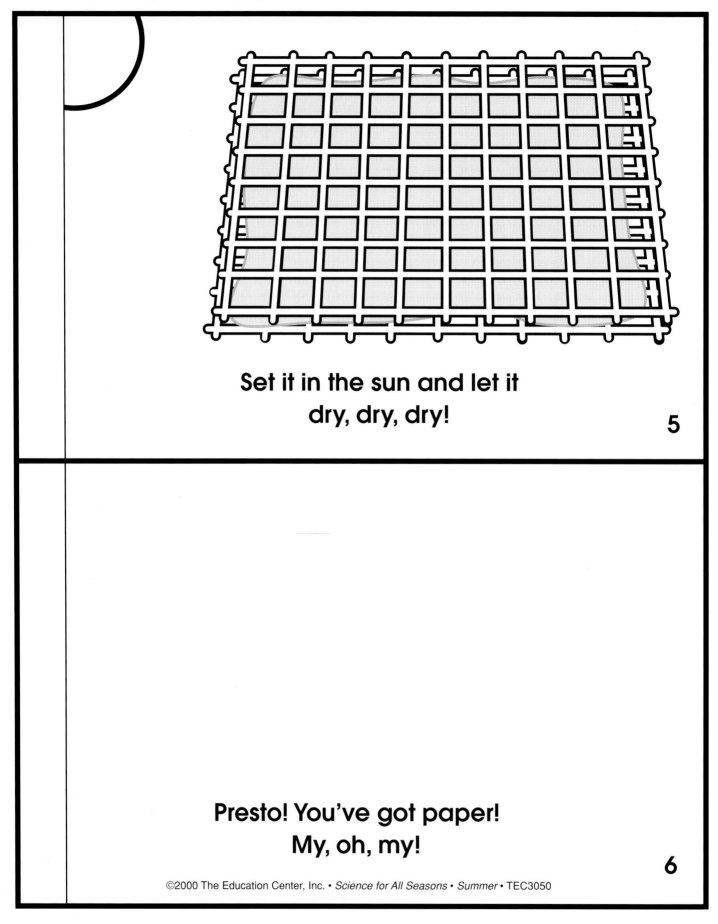

Set it in the sun and let it
dry, dry, dry!

5

Presto! You've got paper!
My, oh, my!

6